START A REVIVAL IN YOUR CITY

Army of the Lord Training Manual

"An Inspiring and Practical Manual"

God's Biblical Strategy for Igniting Revival in Your Life and Your City

BY

KARYL GAEHRING

Copyright © 2022

All rights reserved. No portion of this book may be reproduced, stored in a retrieval system, or transmitted in any form of or by any means – electronic, mechanical, photocopy, recording, scanning, or other – except for brief quotations in critical reviews or articles, without the prior written permission of the publisher. Permission is granted to copy the "Oath of Commitment" found on page 169 in the back of the book.

All Scripture quotations, unless otherwise indicated are taken from the following:

King James Version ®, Copyright © 1982 by Thomas Nelson, Inc. Used by permission All rights reserved.

NKJV Study Bible copyright © 1997, 2007, by Thomas Nelson, Inc. Used by permission.

Scripture taken from THE MESSAGE. Copyright © 1993, 1994, 1995, 1996, 2000, 2001, 2002. Used by permission of NavPress Publishing Group.

Scripture quotations marked TPT are from the Passion Translation ® Copyright © 2017, 2018 by Passion & Fire Ministries, Inc. Used by permission. All rights reserved. ThePassionTranslation.com.

Scripture quotations noted NLT are from the Holy Bible, NEW LIVING TRANSLATION, copyright @ 1996. Used by permission of Tyndale House Publishes, Inc., Wheaton, Illinois 60189. All rights reserved.

ISBN 9798811728879

CONTENTS

INTRODUCTION —9

CHAPTER 1 —14
CALL TO ARMS —14
- DEFINITION —14
- GOD'S SCRIPTURAL BLUEPRINT —16
- START A REVIVAL IN YOUR CITY! —19

CHAPTER 2 —22
ENLISTING IN GOD'S ARMY —22

CHAPTER 3 —32
BASIC TRAINING —32
- CONCERNING GOOD AND EVIL —39
- BATTLE LINES OF THE INVISIBLE WAR —43
- KNOW SATAN'S TACTIC'S —44
- SATAN'S STRATEGIES —45

CHAPTER 4 —47
BOOT CAMP —47

CHAPTER 5 —54
STRATEGIZING THE ENEMY'S TERRITORY —54
- SPIRITUAL WARFARE —56
- TWO SPIRITUAL WARFARES —56
- THE INVISIBLE WAR —56
- THREE AREAS THIS MAY OCCUR —57
- STRATEGIES IN SPIRITUAL WARFARE —59
- LEARN THESE SCRIPTURES —60
- SURPRISE ATTACKS —62
- COMMUNICATION —63
- UNIFORMS —64
- HONOR ALL RANKS IN THE ARMY OF THE LORD —67

CHAPTER 6 —68
GOD'S BATTLE STRATEGY —68

CHAPTER 7 —72
EQUIPPING THE SOLDIER —72

CHAPTER 8 —79
THE WAR ROOM —79

CHAPTER 9 — 88
SPIRITUAL WARFARE — 88
SCRIPTURAL STRATEGIES FOR DEFEATING THE ENEMY — 91
FASTING — 91
WHILE FASTING WE NEED TO — 92
THE WORD OF GOD — 94
DELGATED POWER AND AUTHORITY — 95
POWER OVER THE ENEMY — 95
FASTING AND PRAYER MUST ACCOMPANY EVERY EVENT — 96
HEALING THE SICK — 97

CHAPTER 10 — 98
MOBILIZING THE ARMY OF THE LORD — 98
DEFENSIVE WARFARE — 99

CHAPTER 11 — 106
GOD'S STRATEGY FOR AN ABUNDANT HARVEST — 106

CHAPTER 12 — 116
BOOTS ON THE GROUND — 116
MOBILIZATION — 116
GENERATION Z AND MILLENNIAL ARSENAL — 119
EQUIPPING SOLDIERS WITH TOOLS — 121
HOW TO REACH OUR CULTURE WITH THE GOSPEL? — 122

CHAPTER 13 — 128
REAPING THE HARVEST — 128
WORSHIP-WORSHIP-SPIRITUAL WARFARE — 131
SPIRITUAL PEP RALLY — 132
WORSHIP — 133
WORD — 133
WARFARE — 134
REHEARSAL — 134

CHAPTER 14 — 138
GOD INVASION - RELEASING REVIVAL — 138
THE LAND REFRESHED — 138
A CALL TO REPENTANCE — 139
GOD'S SPIRIT POURED OUT — 140

CHAPTER 15 — 143
"A CHRISTIAN REVIVAL REVOLUTION" — 143

- CREATE IN ME A CLEAN HEART --- 144
- REVIVAL -- 152

CHAPTER 16 -- **158**

WALKING IN THE SUPERNATURAL POWER OF GOD --------------------- **158**

- SIGNS --- 158
- WONDERS -- 159
- MIRACLES -- 159
- GIFTS OF THE HOLY SPIRIT -- 159
- HEALINGS -- 160
- THE OATH OF COMMITMENT -- 169

MORE ABOUT THE AUTHOR --- **171**

- WE WOULD LOVE TO HEAR FROM YOU -------------------------------- 177
- OTHER BOOKS AVAILABLE --- 178
- KARYL GAEHRING IS AVAILABLE TO SPEAK ------------------------- 179

INTRODUCTION

You have a tool in your hand that will provide God's Biblical Strategy for activating a fresh move of God and tremendous revival in your city. Many scriptures are presented throughout this book to give strong biblical principles for a spiritual revolution to transform any community, and to Start A Revival in Your City. We know it is "not by might, nor by power, but by My Spirit, says the Lord of hosts." (Zechariah 4:6 NKJV)

When the Covid-19 pandemic hit all over the world in 2020, restaurants, businesses, schools, churches, and countless other entities were forced to shut their doors. Thousands of people lost their jobs, countless numbers lost their lives, the economy dropped, and the gas and food prices went sky high everywhere. The reports were endless and devastating.

Most church doors were closed and because of this many resolved to having their services online. For a while they were able to sustain their regular attendance and even gained new people. But as time passed and the pandemic lasted much longer than everyone had anticipated, many pastors and leaders noticed a decline in their attendance, and their finances began to drop. There were a few that were able to move forward while others discovered that some of their faithful members while surfing the internet, had found other churches and some of their people moved on. Sad to say many smaller churches did not survive and had to shut their doors permanently.

Today, pastors and leaders in churches and ministries all over the world are struggling to gain new members and retrieve some of

INTRODUCTION

the people they lost in that unexpected and unplanned for event. Reports

of pastors being discouraged due to the fact that they seemingly were unable to gain back many of those they had lost, began working feverishly to survive the bedlam that Covid-19 created in their church and or ministries.

This book is written with the intention of giving you a God-given Biblical Strategy and a fresh new perspective. "Do not remember the former things, nor consider the things of old. Behold, I will do a NEW thing, now it shall spring forth Shall you not know it?" (Isaiah 43:18-19 NKJV) Another version simplifies it this way, "Forget about what's happened; don't keep going over old history. Be alert, be present. I'm about do something brand-new. It's bursting out, don't you see it? " (Isaiah 43:18-19 MSG). When God said, "Do not remember the former things, nor consider the things of old", the literal interpretation means we can remember those things God did, but here is the key, "Forget HOW He did them." Why is that? Because we would limit God and hinder the flow of His plan for the 'new." He desires to do a NEW THING!

I believe the last few decades have been a season of God "setting up" for God to "show up." We have learned and gained so much knowledge and have become very educated in the Word, and all this has been for a purpose, "for such a time as this." (Esther 4:14 NKJV)

Our nation is in desperate need of our Savior, the Lord Jesus Christ. We see that the 'world' is not coming into the church. Matter of fact, there has been a tremendous decline in church growth everywhere. Perhaps they have turned away due to disturbing things they have witnessed and observed in the church world, or by church people's posts they have seen or read on social media. They obviously have a very negative feel of Christianity

INTRODUCTION

and the church, or in their terms, "religion". They have seen enough hypocrisy via comments, debates, and other things they have witnessed in response to their worldly comments, by some well-meaning believers who have no tact, training, or teaching in the basic principle of how to approach an unsaved person, or how to witness to someone in a way that does not send them off running in the opposite direction. People in the world have observed actions and reactions to their ungodly or unholy way of living, which by the way, is the often the way many unbelievers act, right? So in their eyes, to see people who profess to be a Christian, but are no different than they are, why should they listen, or even want to become one, much less enter the doors of a church?

Others have lived in homes where their parents lived a very different lifestyle then the one they presented in the church on Sundays, and have chosen not to duplicate the actions of their hypocritical parents by rejecting church, church friends, and retreating to their unsaved friends. Then there are those who have never been loved or raised in a home where they have been nurtured, cared for, and respected. Please do not feel I am judging or being critical, I am trying to present to you how the unsaved person perhaps sees things, and why they have turned away from the church. Obviously, there are many more reasons than this, but hoping to bring understanding and more clarity so we can reach a world that is lost and to those who have no hope.

Our desire is to see revival fires lit in cities all over the world. We are giving you strong biblical truths, tools, and guidelines that will assist you in this midnight hour, before the Lord returns to see souls saved and see new people come into your ministry.

Reaching the lost and seeing lives changed and transformed should be our number one desire. We believe as you reach them they will come and plug into your local church and ministries to be nurtured, loved, and discipled by you. When new people catch the

INTRODUCTION

fire of God in their spirit, they bring into your ministry new zeal, and a fire that spreads all throughout your church, overflows into the community and out into the city. When the fire of God consumes them it has tremendous potential to spread everywhere.

When people truly become born again in a real conversion, there is a radical change in the life of an individual and their story today can go viral. When the wind of God's Spirit begins to blow it only takes a spark for a fire to spread. When this begins to happen, you will witness evidence in your city. Crime and murder rates go down, abusive relationships healed and restoration of families, drug and alcohol addictions greatly decline, along with so many other things.

Of course, prayer is the key, yes, but the word also says, "Faith without works is dead." We have sought the Lord for His Biblical Strategy concerning the new thing He speaks of in Isaiah 43:19 NKJV. "Behold I do a new thing, and now it will spring forth; shall you not know it?" Prayers are powerful! As your people begin to go out into the fields and reap the harvest, and as you begin to see multiplication take place in your church or ministry, expect to see an authentic move of God break out in your church, community, and your city. When it does, it then has the potential to spread through the state, and spill over into the nation, and even globally. God has promised this found in Habakkuk 2:14 NKJV. "For the earth will be filled with the knowledge of the glory of the Lord, as the waters cover the sea". May you find this book to be a powerful tool to start a revival in your city and may you be among many others that want to set their city and then their world on fire for God. Start a Revival in YOUR City!

Respectfully Submitted,

Karyl Gaehring

INTRODUCTION

CHAPTER 1
CALL TO ARMS

Definition

"To protect against a takeover, an invitation or appeal to undertake a distinct course of action, a command for a group of people to fight against the enemy. Something that makes people come together for a specific result."

"And from the days of John the Baptist until now the kingdom of heaven suffers violence, and the violent take it by force." (Matthew 11:12 NKJV)

There is a great war being raged in the world today. Some consider this a conflict between nations and governmental leaders. However, there is an invisible war that is taking place in the spirit world not visible to the natural eye. The word clearly tells us, "But you, beloved, building yourselves up in your most holy faith, pray in the power of the Holy Spirit." (Jude 1:20 NLT) Now more than ever we need to come together as one and pull down the strongholds of the enemy. Prayer is the key but "faith without works is dead." (James 2:20 NKJV)

Did you know that military terminology is used throughout the New Testament? The early church viewed conflict in their spiritual experience in terms of warfare. The Word of God is compared to a sword. Scripture tells us to "Put on the whole armor of God, that you may be able stand against the wiles of the devil. For we do not

Chapter 1   CALL TO ARMS

wrestle against flesh and blood, but against principalities, against powers, against the rulers of the darkness of this age, against spiritual hosts of wickedness in the heavenly places. Therefore, take up the whole armor of God, that you may be able to withstand in the evil day, and having done all, to stand." (Ephesians 6:11-13 NKJV) Satan's attacks were called 'fiery darts." They "fought the good fight." Today Satan has intensified his attacks against the church, and too many churches have withdrawn from the front lines.

Apostle Paul warned us in the end times we are to know spiritual warfare. "But know this, that in the last days perilous times will come For men will be lovers of themselves, lovers of money, boasters, proud, blasphemers, disobedient to parents, unthankful, unholy, unloving, unforgiving, slanderers, without self-control, brutal, despisers of good, traitors, headstrong, haughty, lovers of pleasure rather than lovers of God, having a form of godliness, but denying its power..." (II Timothy 3:1-5 NKJV)

Revival is in the heart of many believers today. Much prayer and intercession has covered the whole earth for many decades. We know that prayer is the key to revival both in the past, present, and future. If you have studied the revivals of the past, such as "Through A Tiffany Window Revival" that took place in Pitman Grove, N.J., to "The Wales Revival", you will also know that there were history making revivalists such as Evan Roberts, David Brainerd, William J. Seymour who began the Azusa Street Revival, Francis Asbury, George Whitefield, John Wesley, and Jonathan Edwards just to name a few. We also know there were those who were powerful evangelists birthed out of tremendous prayer lives such as Smith Wigglesworth, Kathryn Kuhlman, Oral Roberts, and Revivalist/Evangelist Steve Hill and John Kilpatrick both known for the Brownsville Revival in Pensacola Florida. All of these revivals and moves of God always had a foundation of serious,

Chapter 1   CALL TO ARMS

consistent, and intense times of prayer and fasting. Each revivalist and evangelist were tremendous intercessors that spent hours of time in their prayer closets each day. They were devoted and dedicated to seeing a revival in their cities and God did not disappoint.

Many believers are waking up from their slumber of comfortable Christianity and realizing that we are in a battle. In the days ahead, I believe that we will see and experience a revival that will break through the great darkness in many nations unlike any we have ever witnessed. The Lord will rise upon His people and display His power in unprecedented ways. But if you are looking for a revival like you may have read about, witnessed, or experienced in the past you are in for a surprise, because God is doing a NEW THING and it remains yet to be seen what that is going to look like.

GOD'S SCRIPTURAL BLUEPRINT

After fasting and seeking God for several months, late one night after praying again I said, "God, I do not know how to start a revival? None of us really do. You have spoken that You will be doing a "new thing" and have told us not to revert to the old way. I need to know YOUR strategy for this coming revival. I laid down on my bed and as soon as my head hit the pillow, He clearly reiterated those three words to me, "God's Biblical Strategy". I thought…'that is it'! I need to know "God's Biblical Strategy" for this "new" move of God that you are desiring to release around the world. "Do not remember the things of old. Behold, I will do a new thing, now it shall spring forth; shall you not know it?" (Isaiah 43:18-19 NKJV) I jumped up and grabbed a pen and paper and began to take notes. This book is the result of what I feel He spoke so clearly.

End Times are upon us and it has never been more obvious then it is now. Studies reveal that Millennials and GenZer's are turning away from religion in order to live out their personal values and beliefs. We need to be researching their generational needs, and reaching out in ways that are relevant, so we can effectively reach all of them. We will be discussing ways later in this book.

We are facing and fighting real wars like we have never fought in our lifetime. We have the legalization of gay marriages, abortion protests, homosexuality, unisex public restrooms, transgender rights, numerous school shootings, and protests that we all have watched in Portland, New York, Seattle, and Philadelphia burning building after building, destroying businesses, flipping over police cars, destroying and setting them on fire, all in which are directly related to out of control crime in the city streets.

Church, it is time to RAISE UP AN ARMY OF THE LORD!!!! It is time for us to lay down our differences and come together to fight this war that is before us. Let us all "get on the same page" and learn to take biblical principles and fight this battle as one unified force. God has forewarned us that, "This is what I will do in the last days – I will pour out my Spirit on everybody…." (Acts 2:17 TPT) Time is running short and His desire is to bring as many into the Kingdom of God before He returns. He has already revealed through scripture of what those times would look like, and what to expect, and what we will need to do. That time is upon us now. We must obey and follow His blueprints for Revival.

Our Commander-in Chief has clearly stated that as soldiers of the cross we are to "So the master told him, 'All right. Go out again, and this time bring them all back with you. Persuade the beggars on the streets, the outcasts, even the homeless. Insist that they come in and enjoy the feast so that my house will be full." (Luke 14:23 TPT) When Jesus clearly told us that the "The harvest is huge and ripe! But there are not enough harvesters to bring it all in." (Matthew 9:37 TPT) this is the cry from our Heavenly Fathers heart! He is asking us, "Whom shall I send, and who will go for us?" Will we reply? (Isaiah 6:8 NKJV) "Lord, here am I, Send Me!" as Isaiah did in that passage?

"Multitudes, multitudes are waiting in the valley of decision." (Joel 3:14) This implies heavily that there are people ready and waiting to make a decision but someone has to tell them. Let us answer, "Yes Lord, we will go! We will go forth as laborers into the harvest field and win the lost, see people revived, restored, renewed and refreshed in their relationship to God."

We will send troops and release our soldiers into our city, and into cities all across the land. We will march together as soldiers of Christ, united to reach our communities, impact our cities, and bring them into the Kingdom of God.

God's blueprint is for our troops from cities everywhere to network together with other cities, and join hands across the land, and see a massive authentic move of God burst into flames of revival that will move across America and into the utter most parts of the world. The Army of the Lord bonding together will display a visual of a unified body of Christ that will bring great glory to God. Soldiers of Christ, we must go and take back what the enemy has stolen from us in all of our cities.

Can you see what will happen when churches and ministries in cities around the world start to raise up 'Armies of the Lord' in their city? Think of the souls that will be won to the Lord. When God causes a dynamic transformation in their heart and life, they too will join the forces to help turn your communities, towns, or cities upside down for Jesus! There is nothing like a new converted believer who truly receives a divine experience with God to help set your church or ministry on fire for God! What a powerful thing this will speak to nations, for the world to see the body of Christ rise up as an Army of the Lord together and turn communities, cities, and nations to God! God is our Commander-in-Chief and the Holy Spirit is the unifying force that will pull all the troops together. It only takes one city to light the fire. Will yours be the one?

Fires catch, fires spreads, and fires can get out of control as well. Where there is a fire spectators are drawn to see what is on fire and watch what is burning. Think what will happen when our nation catches this fire of God? Together we work to raise up troops in the Army of the Lord and release them into cities all over America and around the world. They will also set fires, a different kind of fire, God's transforming, spiritual fires, and together we release the fire of God to spread throughout the land.

START A REVIVAL IN YOUR CITY!

Be encouraged to set your people, your church, ministry, or home group on fire in soul winning. Send them out into the marketplace, into schools and colleges, and into the work place. Pastors and leaders' reach out in your church and raise up a whole army involving as many people as you can to reach every age group. Involve everyone!!! If the older generation is unable to go out often, they are great prayer warriors. Ask them to be praying in the "War Room" at a designated place and time together. Give them specifics written down as the Army of the Lord goes out to win the lost so they know exactly what to pray for. Ask them to pray the whole time the Army of the Lord is out fighting the battle. Remind them to be like Aaron who held Moses arms up during battle. As long as Aaron held Moses arms up, they would win, but when the arms dropped down, they started losing. (Exodus 17:12-14 NKJV) God was revealing to all of us how important prayer is during the battle. They too are soldiers and this is a very crucial part to winning the battle. Everyone is pulling together to see change transpire in the hearts of those in the community.

There will be some who would love to support parents who would like to be involved in the Army of the Lord and be like grandparents to their kids during the time of the training classes. Also, they could teach, play games, and have crafts for the children when the parents go out into the combat zone. Note: Some of those in this generation will want to be involved in the "War Room" prayer, intercession, and spiritual warfare sessions. Others will want to sign up for an hour to assist with the children, and there will be some who would like to do both. By dividing the time up to just an hour with each set of grandparents with the kids, they still can be involved in the War Room prayer time as well. All are a vital part of the Army of the Lord.

It could also fill a void for some in this generation who may feel they have lost their place in the church. We suggest rotating the older couples throughout the night so no one in this generation is overly burdened with too heavy a responsibility with other children. Using three couples, one couple could do one hour of fun games, the second couple could teach an hour of bible stories, and the third couple take the last hour and have a movie night with popcorn and drinks, each couple serving in the children's area just one hour. This brings everybody working together in the church or ministry to win your community and see a revival in your city. Everyone feels a part and everyone is involved in some way. It bonds a church and ministry together for a powerful revival in your city.

Think what God can do if pastors and leaders taught this as a 'series' to the people in your church, ministry, or home group. You will begin to see your people winning the lost and getting excited about it. As they do, watch God pour out His fresh anointing on your ministry as they begin take your city over for His Kingdom?

I encourage you to start by leading your people in a fast. Ask them to pray diligently and seek God. Gather as many as you possibly can to pray for those who need Jesus. Every soldier must be involved in this very important time. Have everyone write down names of family member, friends in schools and colleges, co-workers, and all those they will be encountering while out on the harvest field. Pray for every soldier that will be going out into the harvest. Pray that God will anoint them, and give them the right words to say. Lay the names they have written down on the altar, and cry out in their behalf. This is one of the most important times you have as pastors and leaders to pull everybody together. This moves the heart of God and helps in unifying your people. After prayer, have someone gather up all the names and put them in a basket. Keep them. Pray over them every time you meet, and add more names as you go along.

When you begin to move forward and reap the harvest, watch what will happen in your ministry, in your community, and in your city. Revival will come because Jesus is contagious! And when He sets your people on fire for reaching and winning your community, and it captures the heart of people who are lost in your community, the spirit of God begins to move, and it soon spills over into your city. Your church people will catch the fire and a new zeal of God will consume them, and it will burst into flames of revival.

CHAPTER 2
ENLISTING IN GOD'S ARMY

"And it shall be, when you hear the sound of marching in the tops of the mulberry trees, then you shall advance quickly. For then the Lord will go out before you to strike the camp of the Philistines"(II Samuel 5:24 NKJV)

God spoke of armies in the Word often. Armies did not just suddenly happen there was organization and structure to them. The armies in the natural world have an induction process of specific things you are required to do in order to join the forces.

Are You Ready to become a part of the ARMY OF THE LORD?

In the first chapter you learned about the invisible war in the spiritual world. In this chapter you will learn how to enlist in the Army of the Lord. In the natural world, armies usually have an induction procedure in which a prospective soldier must participate in order to join the forces. The induction period makes them part of the army.

God has a very special plan for induction through which you become part of His spiritual army. His plan centers on two important concepts, repentance and conversion, which result in the action of declaring or being made right in the sight of God.

In the natural world when a soldier joins an army, they must deny any previous allegiance they have had to another army or country. When you join the Army of the Lord, you must repent of your allegiance to sin and the kingdom of Satan. This is done by repentance. Repentance is an inward decision or change of mind resulting in the outward action of turning from your sin or a sinful lifestyle to God, and to giving your full self to His right standards of living. (Acts 20:21 NKJV) calls it "repentance toward God and faith toward our Lord Jesus Christ." By this act of repenting, and meaning it from the depths of your heart, you turn away from your sin and you leave the kingdom of Satan. Repentance is a personal decision to change your alliance from the kingdom of darkness and Satan, to the kingdom of light and God. By doing this from a sincere heart, this change of mind and turning from your evil ways and sin cannot be done in yourself. It is the power of God that actually brings the change in your mind and in your lifestyle. This is proof that your allegiance is no longer to Satan, but now to God.

How do you enlist in the Army of the Lord? In the natural Army you would speak with a recruiter. Likewise, in the Army of the Lord, you would speak with a person who is in a similar position of acting as a recruiter, and they can help you understand how to join the Army of the Lord and what is required.

People who are in the Army of the Lord can also help direct you to that person. If you are in the beginning stages of setting up an Army of the Lord, then the pastor or leader should appoint specific soldiers to act as recruiters, they will be able to sign people up and explain the procedure so they can understand the requirements.

1. The first requirement is they must be born again and of good reputation.
2. They also must attend classes and complete qualifications found in the 'Oath of Commitment' and sign and date it.

3. If they are coming from another organization they should have a letter from their pastor or leader letting you know they are born again and give a strong reference for them to be a part.

Soldiers are encouraged to recruit people they know who fit the qualifications, to sign up and become a part of the Army of the Lord. The applicant has to meet the obligations stated above.

We take this assignment from the Lord very seriously. We have an "Oath of Commitment." When anyone enlists into the Army of the Lord program we ask that people sign the oath and return it in to the leader. This "Oath of Commitment" can be read below, but will also be found in the back of the book to make copies of to distribute. Here is how the oath reads

"I, _____ have this day, voluntarily enlisted myself, as a soldier, in the Army of the Lord. I commit myself to giving full attention to the teaching and the training provided, and will complete all classes and any class assignments. I commit myself to God and my leaders to take this opportunity seriously. I understand the importance to be fully trained in this program, so that I can be spiritually equipped to be effective in this ministry as unto God. I commit to serve God and His Kingdom in following the guidance and direction of my spiritual leaders in the Army of the Lord. I will commit to living a lifestyle that is pleasing to the Lord, and volunteer my service to help this ministry in any way possible to help usher people into the Kingdom of God. I will support this ministry in every means possible to help further the gospel of the Lord Jesus Christ to see souls saved. I solemnly commit myself before God and this ministry, that I will serve well and faithfully the opportunities of which I am about to enter, so help me God."

Signature_____

Chapter 2 ENLISTING IN GOD'S ARMY

Date_____

    Training provided is about gaining knowledge, understanding, and sharpening our skills, learning the tactics of the enemy, and knowing how to use our spiritual weapons properly, which are all needed to know how to reach the lost generation that is before us.

God's word clearly tells us to "Overcome every form of evil as a victorious soldier of Jesus the Anointed One. For every soldier called to active duty must divorce himself from the distractions of this world so that he may fully satisfy the One who chose him. An athlete who doesn't play by the rules will never receive the trophy so remain faithful to God! The farmer who labors to produce a crop should be the first one to be fed from its harvest. Carefully consider all that I've taught you, and may our Lord inspire you with wisdom and revelation in everything you say and do. But make Jesus, the Anointed One, your focus in life and ministry. For He came to earth as the descendant of David and rose from the dead, according to the revelation of the gospel that God has given me." (II Timothy 2:3-8 TPT)

In order to be properly prepared for these perilous times, renewed emphasis must be placed on the strategies of spiritual warfare. The Christian life is war. The sooner we recognize and prepare for it, the sooner we will experience victory. Apostle Paul explains to us the characteristic of the Last Days. "But you need to be aware that in the final days the culture of society will become extremely fierce. People will be self-centered lovers of themselves and obsessed with money. They will boast of great things as they strut around in their arrogant pride and mock all that is right. They will ignore their own families. They will be ungrateful and ungodly. They will become addicted to hateful and malicious slander. Slaves to their desires, they will be ferocious, belligerent haters of what is good and right. With brutal treachery, they will act without restraint, bigoted and wrapped in clouds of their conceit. They will find their delight in the pleasures of this world more than the pleasures of the loving God. They may pretend to have respect for God, but in reality, they want nothing to do with God's power..." (II Timothy 3:1-5a TPT)

Apostle Paul told us clearly in II Timothy 3 what the signs would be of the Last Days. We discussed in Chapter 1 the great battle being waged in the spiritual world. It is a personal battle within between the flesh and the spirit. It is also a social battle with evil supernatural powers. Today, we are in a spiritual war like no other. This is why the Army of the Lord needs to pull together to fight the onslaught of the enemy and his evil forces. We need to rise up and combat the powers of darkness together.

Spiritual warfare must be studied and understood within God's total purpose for redeeming those who are bound by sin and do not know God. Authority over Satan was given to the disciples before they were sent out to share the Gospel. We are His disciples, and He has given us the same authority found in Matthew 28:18-20 TPT." Then Jesus came close to them and said, "All authority of the universe has been given to Me. Now wherever you go, make disciples of all nations, baptizing them in the name of the Father, the Son, and the Holy Spirit. And teach them to faithfully follow all that I have commanded you. And never forget that I am with you every day, even to the completion of this age." Jesus also told us "Don't worry or surrender to your fear." (John 14:1 TPT)

"I tell you the timeless truth The person who follows me in faith, believing in me, will do the same mighty miracles that I do – even greater miracles than these because I go to be with my Father! For I will do whatever you ask me to do when you ask me in my name. And that is how the Son will show what the Father is really like and bring glory to him. Ask me anything in my name, and I will do it for you!" These are the very words of Jesus to anyone who believes in Him! God is with us and we can rely on Him to be with us, so we need not fear. (John 14:12-14 TPT)

This is a very real war. The enemy will come against us in various ways, but we have authority that God has given us over him and his demonic forces. Always use God's words to combat the enemy. Equipped with the power of the living God, we have all authority given to us by Him, and God has promised us that His word will not return void. "So will the words that come out of my mouth will not come back empty handed. They'll do the work I sent them to do, they'll complete the assignment I gave them." (Isaiah 55:11 MSG).

After a soldier is inducted into God's army, they always receive "Basic Training". Here we learn the battle lines of the invisible war as they are defined. Enemy territory and strategy are identified, and a general overview of God's battle plan is presented.

We will learn teamwork, discipline, and how to handle our spiritual weapons. You will know what to expect and arrive prepared when the time comes to go into combat.

In the natural world no soldier is sent to battle without first going through Basic Training. This training teaches them how to prepare to enter the combat zone.

It is vitally important that we understand that the Lord of Hosts is the "Commander-in-Chief." We have learned that there is a great spiritual battle being waged between the forces of good and evil.

We will begin by learning about the spiritual forces of good. These are the powerful spiritual forces that assist the believers in warfare. Many gods are worshipped throughout the world, but our God is the true God. He will not send us into battle unprepared and not knowing how to fight the evils of this world.

God describes the basic qualities of both His character and His attributes. God the Father, Jesus Christ, and the Holy Spirit. God made a way for all of us to have a 24/7 hotline to heaven. He left the Holy Spirit to be present everywhere, all the time.

(II Chronicles 16:9 NKJV) says "For the eyes of the Lord run to and fro throughout the whole earth..." (Proverbs 15:3 NKJV) "The eyes of the Lord are in every place, beholding the evil and the good."

God knows all things (I John 3:20 NKJV)

God is all-powerful (Psalms 62:11 NKJV)

God is sinless and pure (I Peter 2:22 NLT – Habakkuk 1:13 NLT)

God is fair and impartial in judgment (Deuteronomy 32:4 NKJV)

God is faithful (I Corinthians 1:9 TPT)

God is good, kind, and merciful (Psalm 145:9 NKJV)

God is kind to all mankind (Exodus 34:6-7 NLT)

God is loving (I John 4:7 NKJV)

When we know these attributes and characteristics of God, we can know that He will oversee us, watch over us, and take care of us in the social battle that lies before us.

It is very important that we spend time in the "War Room" seeking the heart of God. When we study the Word of God we get to know about Him, and who He is, and all that He has for us. We find the battle strategy already laid out in God's word, and we become equipped with His word to handle all kinds of various situations that may arise. But spending time in the "War Room", our prayer closet is where God downloads His anointing for the day and for the tasks that lie ahead of us. We all must privately and as a group, spend quality time in prayer, in His presence, and listening to His voice receiving the fresh anointing for the tasks that lie ahead of us both personally, and corporately. Our Worship, The Word, and the War Room go hand in hand and equip us for the fight that lies ahead of us.

Apostle Paul clearly illustrates strenuous duties of a soldier. He emphasizes it is a serious commitment to the Lord, as well as taking the oath as a soldier. God Is not just a taskmaster, but He is a rewarder of those who diligently seeks Him. We will reap the reward of a bountiful harvest. (Hebrews 11:6 NKJV)

Every Christian is called to be a soldier in the Army of the Lord. Soldiers are called to counter the evil, by overcoming evil with good that flows from a heart of love from God. Many people have all kinds of excuses when it comes to evangelism, but many times their excuses may be a direct result of not having been properly trained and equipped. The Bible clearly tells us that we all are to be 'fishers of men.' His word clearly says, "Go YOU into all the world and preach the gospel to every creature."

(Mark 16:15 NKJV) He then goes on in verse 17 and says, "And these signs *will follow those who believe...*" Now it is very clear that this is written to everyone who has been born again. Not just to a pastor, or leader, or evangelist, etc. it is written to everyone.

God has promised us that when we take Him at His Word, He will be right there with us as we venture to win a soul to Christ. He even goes further and says that if we are a believer of His, that signs will literally follow those who believe." (Mark 16:17 NKJV) In other words when we take that step of faith in obedience to His word, He will be right there with us. We are not alone.

Sin is rampant and too many saints are unconcerned or asleep. Cities everywhere are filled with unbelievers and sin is overpowering our communities. Soldiers of the Lord are willing to lay their life down for the One who laid His life down for them and turn a city upside down for Jesus. They will be used to display signs, wonders, and miracles to 'unbelievers' and even 'unbelieving Christians', to validate the fact that He is alive, real, and relevant for today. Pastors and leaders, it is your responsibility to arouse those awake who are asleep and unconcerned who are under your leadership. We will give you the scriptural equipment and biblical principles so you can teach and then experience the wind of God blow fresh and anew upon your people.

God's desire is for you to have a powerful move of God in your city! He wants you to take your city for Christ. How is this going to happen? Individually we must catch God's vision for souls, and for the lost, backsliders, and those who are broken. We don't have to look far.

We must burn with fire and compassion for those who do not know the Lord. When a new convert truly catches a glimpse of Jesus, when they really accept Him fully into their heart, something happens. A visible change occurs. The evidence is all around and witnessed by others and it overflows into a church/ministry, it then trickles down into a community, and it explodes into a city. Revival!

As we move towards preparing for an authentic move of God, we truly believe you will see an invasion of God when we have a passion for God, we become motivated with His love. This is why reading the word of God is essential because again as we read the word we get to know about Him, but when we pray we get to know Him and we fall in love with Him. Once again God reveals His heart when He says, "But I have this against you have abandoned your first love." (Revelation 2:4 TPT) This is a major concern of God. This is another part of revival that comes and moves through the body of Christ. People passionately fall in love with Him all over again.

Every born again believer should recognize that our world is in desperate need for a Savior. Our world needs healing all throughout the land. Another key to revival is this. We will never see it unless we believers come before God and ask Him what we are personally doing that grieves Him. We all know this scripture, "If MY PEOPLE, who are CALLED BY MY NAME will humble themselves, and pray and seek My face, and turn from their wicked ways, then I will hear from heaven, will forgive their sin and heal their land." (II Chronicles 7:14 NKJV) This is the first step for every soldier to fall in love all over again with Jesus. When we truly fall in love with Him, draw close to Him, desire Him above anyone and everything, then we become filled with His compassion. God's compassion in His believers is what is going to win the world. The same kind of compassion that Jesus has and that only He can give.

CHAPTER 3
BASIC TRAINING

"By this we know love, because He laid down His life for us. And we also ought to lay down our lives for the brethren. But whoever has this world's goods, and sees his brother in need, and shuts up his heart from him, how does the love of God abide in him? "(I John 3:16-17 NKJV)

The Army of the Lord is powerful when we march to the orders of our Commander-in- Chief. He has a plan and purpose for every person who comes and gives their life to Him. As the Army of the Lord is growing you will find that together we begin to gain momentum. In the beginning people may have mixed emotions about going out on the streets, or to concerts, spring socials, etc. to reach others. Sometimes you will find that a few people may have concerns about talking to strangers, you may find this often. Most have never been taught so they do not know what to say, nor do they know how to approach someone and start talking with them about Jesus. They are apprehensive because they do not know how to minister to people they do not know. They do not even know how to minister to some they DO know. This is why teaching and training is so important, to take away those uncertainties and uncomfortable feelings.

Maybe you have had outreaches in the past and very few people showed up. We have found that it is not because people do not want to get involved, but it is often because they are afraid to share their faith with anybody. They just do not know how. Some have the mindset of 'that is what the pastor is supposed to do'. No! All God's people are the ones who are called to bring them in. This is the purpose of this whole book is to equip the saints as soldiers in the Army of the Lord. YOU GO! "And he said to them, "As you go into all the world, preach openly the wonderful news of the gospel to the entire human race!" (Mark 16:15 TPT)

There are people in the congregation or audience that sit before you week after week, listen to sermon after sermon, and you do not see them until the following Sunday. Also, as you know, people are extremely busy these days, have multiple responsibilities, so a suggestion would be to make this opportunity almost like a campaign out of your teaching, letting them know, this is what our goal is as a church to win our city, to see a revival break out right here. So we will need as much participation from every age group as possible. Make your plans to be a part of the biggest event our church, ministry, or home group has ever done. Our communities have a need, many are lost, our city is desperate for a vital move of God. Every empty chair or pew in this room represents a person in our city who will be sitting here with us. It will take all of us working together to raise up an Army of the Lord and take back what the devil has stolen from us! Let's come together as a mighty Army of the Lord and win your co-workers, your school and college friends, people in our post offices, banks, grocery stores, and everywhere the people are. Together we can make a difference!

As the pastor or leader, we highly suggest having banners in your hallways, videos for announcements, people dressed in their uniform to come on the platform, consistently giving exposure to your Army of the Lord Ministry. Ask them to briefly share with the people what it means to them to be in the Army of the Lord. Have them invite people to come and be a part. Promote it. Arouse people's curiosity, keep it in front of them, teach it, preach it, talk about it as our Big Day for our Big Event, giving them dates, day, and time. This provides a definite goal and creates excitement and enthusiasm to finish the course. Prepare for this to be ongoing.

Lock down a place in a good location prior to having your big event. We encourage it to be outside of your church or ministry, a neutral place that everyone is familiar with, where people will come. The church facility or building is not recommended because non-believers feel you may be pressuring them to come to your church and will not attend the event. Once you reach them and their hearts are changed they will want to become a part of your church.

Months prior to the Big Event, the Army of the Lord will have gone out regularly and will have talked with people and won some to the Lord. Set up times for the youth who are in involved in the Army of the Lord to go out invite people in their schools, friends, etc. They can go door-to-door and hand out flyers inviting people to come to the event. You could give out free water at stoplights and hand them a flyer. Get the word out! Have ads on TV, radio, and in newspapers at least six weeks in advance. God has big plans for your city and that is a massive revival!!!

People will come, souls will be saved, and you must be prepared for the harvest. Be ready in your church or ministry to teach those who will be coming in. Know that you will be receiving many unchurched people, those who have no or very little knowledge of God's word.

1. First, teach them 'how' to pray. They do not know how. When they learn how and start seeing answers to their prayers, then they want to learn more about the Bible. I have a very simple but profound book called "PRAYER POWER" available on Amazon. This teaches people how to pray and it is very easy reading and effective.

2. Have classes ready to teach and train the newcomers. Love them. Invite them in. Have Bible studies appropriated right to them. Soldiers can also help in these areas.
3. Have a luncheon just for them to meet people in our church or ministry or home group community. You will have to raise these new babes up in Christ. Starting from scratch. Love, love, love them. (I Corinthians 13 MSG)
4. Make soldiers out of them. Let them go through the training to become a Soldier in the Army of the Lord. This is not a one-time revival. God wants this to be on going until He comes to take us home.
5. Reach them, teach them, train them, equip them, and in everything you do love them. God has given us a huge responsibility, but He has given us everything we need to usher in a revival and sustain it to Jesus returns.

Maybe you have never thought what it would be like if you could motivate the majority of your people to be soul winners? What would it be like if you taught them and trained them how to lead their co-worker to Jesus? What would it be like for them to come in to your service and give testimonies how they led someone to the Lord at a gas station or grocery store? What would happen if a soldier prayed for someone in a grocery store and they were healed? What would it be like if your ministry caught this kind of fire and began to burn for the Lord in your city?

You have the means, the Word, power through prayer, and the people to be able to literally raise up an Army of the Lord right there in your church and ministry to reach your town, your city. You may say, but where does it say this in the Bible? Let me give you some scriptures to help you get a visual where you will be able to see in God's word that He speaks about the very word "army' numerous times in the Word.

"The LORD gives voice before His army, For His camp is very great; for strong is the One who executes His word. For the day of the LORD is great and very terrible; who can endure?" (Joel 2:11 NKJV)

"Blessed be the Lord, my rock, who trains my hand for war, and my fingers for battle." (Psalm 144:1 NKJV)

"Then David said to the Philistine, "You come to me with a sword, a spear, and a javelin, but I come to you in the name of the Lord of hosts, the God of the armies of Israel, who you have taunted." (I Samuel 17:45 NKJV)

"The number of army of the horsemen were two hundred million; I heard the number of them." (Revelation 9:16 NKJV)

You can see, it is God's idea and strategy to raise up an Army of the Lord. David said "You've trained me with the weapons of warfare-worship, now I'll descend into battle with power to chase and conquer my foes. You empower me for victory with your wraparound presence. Your power within makes me strong to subdue, and by stooping down in gentleness you strengthened me and made me great. You've set me free from captivity and now I'm standing complete, ready to fight some more! I caught up with my enemies and conquer them, and didn't turn back until the war was won!" (Psalm 18:34-37 TPT) He goes on to say in verse 39, "You've placed your armor upon me and defeated my enemies, make them bow low at my feet." "You gave me victory on every side." (Verse 4:3a TPT)

There are many more scriptures that talk about the armies of the Lord. Many leaders are concerned about the 'growth of the church", they talk about how Covid-19 has played havoc in their ministry, and how many have still not returned. I am sure you do

Chapter 3 BASIC TRAINING

know that many people all around you do not go to church anywhere. You know there are people around you who will never go to church unless someone reaches them and then invites them to come.

The Army of the Lord is all about learning teamwork and techniques about how to win our city for Jesus. People are interested. You can ask, 'would you like to be a part?' You may start out with a small group and that is okay. As they get uniforms and start to share the excitement, others around them begin to catch the vision and often desire to become a part too.

Have you ever thought about the people who attend your services who would get involved if they knew 'how' to talk to someone, "how" to approach a stranger, and if they knew what to say? If you raise up an Army of the Lord in your church or ministry, it will inspire others to get involved.

We have found that when we begin to share the idea of reaching our city and how we plan to do it people get enthused and excited about it. When I wear my uniform that is simply green camo pants, a green army hat, and my God Invasion 'Army of the Lord' T-shirt, people come up to talk and ask questions and it leads to an invite. I ask them if they know of anyone who they know, or church group that would be interested in joining us in starting a revival in their city? Also, we suggest they invite them to come to our 'War Room". Then they ask, what is the "War Room?" They may say, I have seen the movie but…" It leads right into what we are doing. We explain that our "War Room" is about prayer. We pray and learn prayer on all levels. Examples are how to pray effectively, how to remove hindrances in our personal lives so that the answers will come, strategic intercession, and so much more. We invite them to come and be a part. We then explain that The Army of the Lord is all about learning teamwork and techniques about how to win our city for Jesus. People are interested. Ask them, "would you like to be a part?"

You may start out with a small group. That is completely fine. As soldiers start getting their uniforms, excitement starts to build. From there you move it to your congregation, or group meeting. Let them know as long as people are born again they are welcome, they can invite people from other churches, and assure them that you are not interested in proselyting but you are about building together the Kingdom of God. Once you have several people who are a part, ask them to wear their uniform on Sunday and have them join you on the platform and let the people know you are building together an Army of the Lord and the goal is to take back what the enemy has stolen from us. Together we will "Start A Revival in Our City!" Promote it. Let people share their stories of what the class is doing for them, and share any videos available on your website where they can watch the classes, or videos of soldiers ministering to people outside of the church, ministry, or home group. Have water baptisms and let the people share their story of where they came from and how they found God and what He means to them now.

By teaching and training your troops, you will watch how God begins to remove their fears and inhibitions from their hearts and minds. An excitement begins to grow and spread throughout your ministry. Together they learn how to deal with their fears, anxieties, apprehensions, and they will learn together to build their confidence in God. They will learn how to lean on Him, and will find that God has gone ahead of them to make the crooked places straight. When you have a troop and you are going out, you will find that each soldier has learned how to approach and befriend people, they have seen how the classes have helped to take the edge off of going out to win the lost. They will become strong as they gain understanding and experience themselves, how they can minister to people one on one effectively. The Army of the Lord builds relationships with others in the church, community, and or home group. The times they come together with others in a scripture and prayer, they grow together spiritually, and when they break up into two's, they will see that they are never alone even when they go out to minister. This helps take the edge off of any concerns they may have.

CONCERNING GOOD AND EVIL

In Basic Training we learn teamwork and discipline, we will learn how to handle our spiritual weapons, we will gain wisdom in how to disarm the enemy, and we will learn how to march to the cadence of the Lord. Our focus is that it is "not by might, it is not by power, but it is by My Spirit says the Lord of hosts." (Zechariah 5:6 NJKV).

With the forces of good we learn that God has provided angels to minister to every individual. The word 'angel' means 'messenger.' Angels are ministering spirits sent by God to do His will. We are assured that "The angel of the Lord encamps around those that fear Him, and delivers them." (Psalm 34:7 NKJV)

The Lord never sends us out alone. We know that we are in an invisible war, serving an invisible God, who provides us with invisible angels. Angels have been known to even talk to people. "Then the angel who had been talking with me returned and woke me, as though I had been asleep. "What do you see now?" he asked? (Zechariah 4:1 NLT)

We will give a few scriptures below that will describe several characteristics of angels that we want you to study on your own. It is important that you thoroughly understand how angels work and their responsibilities. To know that God provides angelic covering for us brings deep peace that we can move forward knowing we are protected. Below are scriptures you can personally study.

- Angels are spirits – (Hebrews 1:14 NKJV)
- Angels have visible and invisible forms - (Numbers 22:22-35 NKJV)
- Angels can appear in the like of human form - (Genesis 19:1-22 NKJV)
- Angels are intelligent - (II Samuel 14 : 20 NKJV)
- Angels are powerful – (Psalm 103:20 NKJV)
- Angels travel at unrecorded speed – (Revelation 8:13, 9:1 NKJV)
- Angels are reverent and their highest honor is to Worship God – (Nehemiah 9:6 NKJV)

These are just to list a few scriptures and their characteristics. There are more that you can research on your own. The word speaks about angels all throughout the Bible. We encourage each soldier to study the scriptures concerning angels and bring them to share with the group. By doing a personal study you will find angelic beings are very involved in God's plans. These are all a part of the good that we as believers have on our side. We need not fear. We cannot see them with our eyes but they are in operation all throughout the day and night. It is very important to know these characteristics about angels. We know that God gives us added invisible protection as we go out as an army to help reach those who are lost and have no hope until they find Jesus.

This is our mission to take Jesus to them. We need to tell them that God wants to be their friend, and that He will eradicate all their sin and give them a fresh new start. He then puts His Spirit in them and gives them the power to change those areas they cannot change on their own.

Angels are active in heaven and on earth, their power is given to them by God, and they are under God's authority.

- They have access to the Presence of God and minister in Heaven in many ways, specifically in worship to God. (Revelation 4:8 NKJV)
- Angels also rejoice over those who accept Jesus as Lord and accept salvation. (Luke 5:10 NLT)
- They also stand ready to do God's will. (Psalm 103:20-21 MSG / NKJV)
- Angels also minister on this earth. They help to strengthen believers. (Luke 22:43 NKJV)
- They minister to believers when they are being tested. (Matthew 4:11 NKJV)
- They guide believers. (Acts 8:26 NKJV).
- Angels also bring answers to prayer. (Danie l9:21-22 NKJV)

When the angels of the Lord are around us they operate in the duties that God has put them over. We know that we can go forth in the Army of the Lord and rest assured that we have tremendous backup for our task.

Other tasks the angels perform

- Angels also warn (Matthew 2:13 NLT)
- They protect (Psalm 91:11 NLT) We have nothing to be afraid of. God oversees us and gives us added protection as we go about our day and especially when we are out doing the work for his kingdom.

It is very important that we understand the coverage that the Lord Himself provides for us are invisible angels. They are very heavily involved in spiritual warfare as well. We truly do not to fear the battle. God sends them to protect us, to provide guidance, and because they move about speedily they bring answers to our prayers. They will warn us and instruct us as well as keep us encouraged. He will send them to deliver us. Angels also intercede and as we all have heard they intervene on the behalf of believers in battle.

If we are ever in danger, we can call on God to dispatch angels to assist us in battle. If we are fearful Psalmist David said, "I sought the Lord and He answered me, and delivered me from all my fears." (Psalm 35:4 NKJV). In that same chapter in verse seven He goes on to say, "The angel of the Lord encamps around those who fear Him, and delivers them." (Psalm 34:7 NKJV)

We are the Army of the Lord. He has given and will continue to give us all the protection we need when we go forth in His name doing His work. It is good to know that we have an invisible force working with us, and the Holy Spirit inside of us, and angels around us. We really have nothing to fear.

- We do not need to be afraid. "For he will order his angels to protect you wherever you go." (Psalm 91:11 NLT)

More important principles we need to remember as soldiers, when out in the combat zone.

- We do need to use wisdom "Don't turn your back on wisdom, for she will protect you. Love her, and she will guard you. Getting wisdom is the wisest thing you can do." (Proverbs 4: 6-7 'NLT)
- We need to be very discerning (II Timothy 2:7 NJKV)
- "Think about what I am saying. The Lord will help you understand all these things." (II Timothy 2:7 NLT)

When you begin training new people you will be working with volunteers. Some will come to you saying they have already been 'trained' from maybe another ministry, or studies they have done on their own. However, they still need to go through the training you will be providing through this book. It is extremely important that everyone goes through the same training so that we all operate

Chapter 3 BASIC TRAINING

under the same teaching and work together as one. We do not want to be disjointed with someone who wants to just jump in. EVERYONE must be taught and operate as an army where all have received the same instruction. Just as a natural army has very strict guidelines, more so should we as the Army of the Lord.

As we work as a team together, we learn as a team together. We learn the fundamentals of soldiering. Much of the training will be in the classroom, or some may offer training on videos, or on Zoom calls. Our time together will be towards working together as a might Army of the Lord.

We also will be focusing on our spiritual weapons. We must be spiritually fit, and we do this by studying the word, and praying individually daily. Do not let your armor down. That is a tactic of the enemy and he loves to come in when you are in a weakened state spiritually, Stay Fit, spiritually and physically. Be faithful in attending all services your church or ministry has to offer, in addition to your own private and personal time with the Lord daily!

BATTLE LINES OF THE INVISIBLE WAR

We have talked about the forces of good, now we will learn concerning the forces of evil. We must know how to identify, track, and target the evil forces and engage targets with our spiritual weapons. We will develop important skills, which include self-discipline, and we will follow it with field training as we progress along.

The Bible teaches us "we must be 'wise' of Satan's schemes". This is so he does not gain advantage over us. We must not be ignorant of his devises. (II Corinthians 2:11 NKJV). We are to be alert and of sober mind. "Your enemy the devil prowls around like a roaring lion looking for someone to devour." (I Peter 5:8 NKJV).

The soldier first knows how to identify the enemy before entering the battlefield. We must constantly remind ourselves of the fact that we are in an invisible war. Always keep that in mind because we are not fighting against people, but we are fighting against the powers of darkness. Attention soldiers, "PUT ON the whole armor of God, that you may be able to stand against the schemes of the devil." It is important that we know the enemy and his nature. (Ephesians 6:11 NKJV)

It is so important that we know his nature and his strategies. Military forces spend much time gathering intelligently information about the enemy. We can only do warfare effectively by identifying him and his tactics and by recognizing his strategies.

KNOW SATAN'S TACTIC'S

Satan is a spirit and because of this he also operates in the invisible realm. We know he is the Prince of the power of the air according to Ephesians 2:2 NKJV. From the beginning,

1. He challenges us just as he did Eve. We can expect this when we go out to minister this is one of his favorite tactics. (Genesis 3 NKJV) gives us a detailed look at his tactic.
2. He says to people today, "Did God really say?" He tries to get people to reconsider what they understand God has said in His Word.
3. Another tactic he uses is to try to get people to add their own interpretation to God's word and then try to nullify it. As we are learning his tactics, keep these in mind as you are out ministering in the Army of the Lord.

4. He works overtime at enticing people to sin but making that sin look very appealing. "But each one is tempted when he is drawn away by his own desires and is enticed. Then when desire has conceived it, it gives birth to sin, and sin when it is full-grown, brings forth death." (James 1:14-15 NKJV). Satan will use a

person's own desires against him to entice him/her into the full-blown sin.

Sin is deceptive, divisive, and destructive. These are weapons the enemy uses in arsenal to destroy an individual, husband and wife, family, churches, businesses, and the list goes on. That is why his tactic has to be hit directly with the word of God when evidenced.

God is a great Commander-in-Chief in this warfare. This is why prayer and intercession is so important. As the Commander-in-Chief He is authorized to direct the movements in this invisible military force. He has the full responsibility of protecting and defending the Army of the Lord. His word clearly states, "Be prepared. You're up against far more than you can handle on your own. Take all the help you can get, every weapon God has issued, so that when it's all over but the shouting you'll still be on your feet..." (Ephesians 6:13-17 MSG) God sees behind the enemies' lines. He knows exactly his strategies that will be used. He shares his secret things with those who belong to the Lord our God." (Psalm 25:14 NKJV). God is making mighty warriors of each one who becomes enlisted in the Army of the Lord.

When we become aware of, and know the enemy's tactics, then we can be prepared with God's Word. Memorize scriptures and use God's Word to combat the enemy, God will always win! "I send it out, and it always produces fruit. It will accomplish all I want it to, everywhere I send it." (Isaiah 55:11 NLT)

We are well covered when we go about doing the work of the Lord. As we are in battle to assist more people in coming into God's Kingdom, we can know that we are heavily guarded and protected as we go about the Lord's business.

SATAN'S STRATEGIES

It is wonderful to know that God 'trains your hands for war and your fingers for battle." (Psalm 144:1 NKJV). When we are aware of his strategies then we can strategically plan our maneuvers in a counter attack. Satan blinds unbeliever's minds to keep them from seeing the truth of the gospel. "Satan, who is the god of this world, has blinded the minds of those who don't believe. They are unable to see the glorious light of the Good News. The don't understand this message about the glory of Christ, who is the exact likeness of God."

(II Corinthians 4:4 NLT) He lies, and he hides the truth. These unbelievers are defenseless against the attacks of the demonic powers that are used against them. Tactics he has always used and still uses in our world today are "The lust of the flesh, the lust of the eyes and the pride of life." God fairly warns us, "For all that is in the world-the lust of the flesh, the lust of the eyes, and the pride of life-is not of the Father but is of the world." (I John 2:15 NKJV)

We know that the spirit of this world is in direct opposition of the Holy Spirit. "Now we have received, not the spirit of the world, but the spirit who is of God that we might know the things that have been freely given to us by God." (I Corinthians 2:12 NKJV)

CHAPTER 4
BOOT CAMP

"Then the master said to the servant, 'Go out into the highways and hedges, and compel them to come in, that my house may be filled." (Luke14:23 NKJV)

BOOT CAMP is the introduction to those coming into the Army of the Lord. In this chapter they will learn the fundamentals of reaching their city by bringing in a spiritual harvest.

Pastors and leaders often become discouraged when 'prayer' and 'outreach' are publicly announced inviting their people to participate, and the response is, very few seem to attend. So many of our churches today experience this same disappointing outcome. Let's stop to evaluate some options as to why this may be. We do know that people today are busier than ever with their home and family responsibilities, schools' extracurricular programs, their tremendous job related workload and obligations, as well as other outside activities. These tremendously hinder people from church opportunities and participation. This is a concern for every pastor, leader, and home group coach.

Another perspective to consider as a possibility, (1) Prayer is seldom taught because there seems to be a popular consensus that everybody knows how to pray, so there seems to be little emphasis on teaching and training, and (2) When it comes to an outreach, there is this general mindset in the church world, "well, let the evangelism team or others do the outreach." People in many ministries today brush it off and never think twice about getting involved. Perhaps it is not presented from the leadership other than an announcement, or maybe there is no announcement. Has it ever crossed anyone's mind that the average church member, the new born believer, or sometimes even the seasoned attender really have no clue how to pray effectively regarding seeing answers to their prayers, nor do they know how to lead someone to the Lord? Perhaps the lack of training, or the lack of compassion for lost souls are the greatest culprit.

Since Covid-19, many pastors and leaders have said, "Our church has picked up, but we still have a lot of members that have not returned." This has been an issue in many churches everywhere from time to time. Today it seems to be the norm that people love to church hop. They shop churches trying to find the niche that suits them and their children's needs, understandably so. Pastors and ministry leaders are left with, "What if they do not return?" What if you keep waiting and hoping they will be back, when perhaps they have moved on permanently? As we all know, many have resorted to watching churches and ministries online. They find it convenient, they don't have to get up and rush to get ready and drive to church, so they watch online. Though most leaders encourage people to physically attend with the scripture that says, "not forsaking the assembling of ourselves together, as is the manner of some, but exhorting one another, and so much the more as you see the Day approaching." (Hebrews 10:25 NKJV) Some have returned but we all know there are reasons why many have not returned, and quite possibly won't.

My question is to pastors, leaders, and home group leaders. Do you have a passion for something new, or do you want to keep going the way you have been? Or do you want something fresh and exciting to open the heart of your city to God who can change, heal, deliver, and set people free? Have you exhausted all of your ideas, methods, and plans? God's heart is for lost souls and for the healing and restoration of people in the body of Christ who also need a new touch. He has said that the "harvest is great, but the workers are few." (Luke 10:2 NLT) Our country is groaning in agony, revealing there is a need to be set free from the strongholds that the enemy of their soul has them trapped in. God also has told us in His word "multitudes, MULTITUDES in the valley of decision." (Joel 3:14 NKJV) What is it going to take to wake us? The answer is for all born again believers to understand that the ball is in our court? He has given us everything that we need to reach those who are empty, hopeless, sick, addicted, depressed, suicidal, and lost!!! This is not just the responsibility of the pastors and leader's; it is OUR responsibility as a believer! How much clearer can the Word be when it says, "Go YOU into all the world..." Everywhere you go there are people who need Jesus. Of course, God can do it, but He has chosen us to help! He is telling us this in Luke 10 and in (Mark 16:15 NLT) "Go into all the world and preach the Good News to everyone."

In BOOT CAMP we will learn the fundamentals of soldiering, the power of teamwork, and the importance of discipline.

One of the first issues that we deal with is fear. Fear is a fundamental factor in many that keeps people from sharing their faith. It is a little word that has a great impact in the heart of many believers. It too often takes a high priority in believer's minds that stops them from telling anyone about their faith and what they believe. Fear, a simple four letter word, is one of the enemies many tactics to keep people from sharing the power saving message to their lost family and friends. Is it our lack of faith in God that causes us to not talk to others about our own personal faith? I don't believe it is. Too many believers have never been given guidance, instruction, teaching and direction in the importance of leading someone to the Lord. They have never been taught how to win a soul to Christ. As pastors and leaders, we are to equip the body of Christ. How can they know if they have never been taught?

Charles Spurgeon, one of the great revivalists of all time once said, "Your one business in life is to lead men to believe in Jesus Christ by the power of the Holy Spirit. Every other thing should be made subservient to this one objective." He also said, "We must thrust the sword of the Spirit into the hearts of men."

We as soldiers must be ready to share Jesus everywhere and at any time or place.

The first thing we must teach every soldier in the Army of the Lord is, they must spend time alone in the Word, and in personal times of prayer daily. They must also be present in the War Room when the whole army comes together. There, our faith is built up, as we open our hearts singing together, praising and worshiping our Commander-in-Chief, receiving a challenging word, and then entering into corporate prayer. The power of God begins to rise in the hearts of all who enter in.

PUT ON THE FULL ARMOR

"Finally, my brethren, be strong in the Lord and in the power of His might. Put on the whole armor of God, that you may be able to stand against the wiles of the devil. For we do not wrestle against flesh and blood, but against principalities, against powers, against the rulers of the darkness of this age, against spiritual hosts of wickedness in the heavenly places. Therefore, take up the whole armor of God, that you may be able to withstand in the evil day, and having done all, to stand. Stand therefore, having girded your waist with truth, having put on the breastplate of righteousness, and having shod your feet with the preparation of the gospel of peace; above all, taking the shield of faith with which you will be able to quench all the fiery darts of the wicked one. And take the helmet of salvation, and the sword of the spirit, which is the Word of God, praying always with all prayer and supplication in the Spirit, being watchful to this end with all perseverance and supplication for all the saints." (Ephesians 6:10-18 NJKV)

The Apostle Paul said, "and for me, that utterance may be given to me, that I may open my mouth boldly to make know the mystery of the gospel, for which I am an ambassador in chains, that in it I may speak boldly as I ought to speak." (Ephesians 6:19-20 NKJV)

We cannot afford to be stationary soldiers who do not advance the gospel to those around us every day. Let us take the following scriptures and break them down into the fundamentals of moving forward as an Army of the Lord.

BE EQUIPPED

We were just told in Ephesians to be equipped. We were told how to dress for war and what weapons and ammunition we are to have on us when we go into the invisible war in the spirit realm. Let's break this down.

Be strong in the Lord

In the POWER of HIS might

PUT ON

The Armor of God

Why are we told to take these steps?

That you may be able to stand against the devils tactics

Always stay attentive

We are not wrestling against people

We are wrestling against an invisible force

Chapter 4 — BOOT CAMP

Satan's beings are invisible - but real

They operate in the unseen realm

Their purpose is to oppose everything

And oppose everyone that belongs to the Lord

Principalities are Satan's angels of darkness

Powers in this verse means delegated influence and authority

TAKE UP YOUR WHOLE ARMOR OF GOD

So you can stand in the evil day

When you have done all these things…

STAND!

OUR PROPER STANCE ONCE WE ARE ARMED

<u>**WEAPONS**</u>

The sword of the Spirit

Shield of Faith

Your shield is so you can quench the fiery darts of the enemy, the wicked one.

Take the helmet of salvation

Take the sword of the Spirit, which is the Word of God

<u>**SPECIAL EMPHASIS ON THE OUR SPIRITUAL WEAPONS**</u>

Your Word I have *HID IN MY HEART*

We must be spiritually fit and properly equipped

Use spiritual discernment always

Discern your territory and turf

Discern people around you

Know how to identify danger and use wisdom

OFFENSIVE STRATEGY

In the natural world armies use both offensive and defensive strategies. Offensive strategy is an aggressive advance against an enemy. We must learn how to defend our territory when the enemy attacks. When sharing the gospel with someone who has never heard it, this is conducting offensive warfare. You are claiming new territory in the name of Jesus.

CHAPTER 5
STRATEGIZING THE ENEMY'S TERRITORY

"Strategic planning is the key to warfare; to win, you need a lot of good counsel." (Proverbs 24:6b MSG)

The military word "strategy" is the word often used for carrying out military operations. It is the God's method or plan that will lead us into victory. As we prepare to raise up an Army of the Lord, spiritual skills and knowledge are necessary as we enter the combat zone, and begin to fight not people, but the invisible enemy and his invisible army. Just as strategies are used in a natural warfare, we must explore the scripture to find the spiritual strategy God has given us to win our world.

This is a tremendous battle we are in that is being waged in the spirit realm. We must clearly understand the battle between the flesh and the spirit. Today we are in a social battle with the evil forces of this world, and it is a spiritual battle with evil supernatural powers. We must remember, "Greater is He that is IN us, then he that is in the world." (John 4:4).

A shofar was used in the Old Testament to call God's people to battle. Today, God's Spirit is releasing a sound in our spirit throughout the nations and all throughout the world. He is calling us to an invisible war and He is giving us an invitation to appeal to undertake a particular course of action to a spiritual "Call to Arms".

Our main verse for this action is found in (Ephesians 6:12-17 TPT). "Your hand-to-hand combat is not with human beings, but with the highest principalities and authorities operating in rebellion under the heavenly realms. For they are a powerful class of demon-gods and evil spirits that hold this dark world in bondage. Because of this, you must wear all the armor that God provides so you're protected as you confront the slanderer, for you are destined for all things and will rise victorious. Put on truth as a belt to strengthen you to stand in triumph. Put on holiness as protective armor that covers your heart. Stand on your feet alert, then you'll always be ready to share the blessings of peace. In EVERY BATTLE, take faith as your wrap-around shield, for it is able to extinguish the blazing arrows coming at you from the evil one. "

In this chapter will reveal the invisible war that every believer is engaged in. It is a war where everyone is the target. As stated we have the natural realm and the spiritual realm. We exist in two worlds when we become born again, we are in both the natural world and the spiritual world. The natural world consists of five senses and they are sight, hearing, touch, smell and taste. It is tangible and visible. The city, nation, or country in which we live in is part of the natural realm. We communicate with people.

However, when you became born again, there is another world in which you live. It is the spiritual world. You cannot see it with your physical eyes, but it is just as real as the natural world in which you live. Apostle Paul says, "There is a natural body, and there is a spiritual body." (I Corinthians 15:40 NKJV) We have a soul and spirit.

SPIRITUAL WARFARE

Spiritual warfare is a spiritual fight between evil verses good. It must be understood with a spiritual mind. It is necessary to use "spiritual discernment" to understand spiritual things. "But the natural man does not receive the things of the Spirit of God; for they are foolishness to him; neither can he know them, because they are spiritually discerned." (I Corinthians 2:14 NKJV)

After Jesus walks on water in (Matthew 14:33 NLT), the disciples tell Jesus, "You really are the Son of God! In response to the question by Jesus, "But who do you say that I am? Peter replied "You are Christ, the Son of the living God." They discerned when they saw visible evidence that Jesus did what no natural man could do.

TWO SPIRITUAL WARFARES

There is a natural kingdom of this world, but there are actually two spiritual kingdoms of this world.

(1) The Kingdom of Satan which consists of Satan himself, spiritual beings called demons, and everyone who lives in sin and rebellion against God's Word.

(2) The Kingdom of God consists of God the Father, Jesus Christ, and the Holy Spirit, spiritual beings called angels, and all the people who live in righteous obedience to God's Word. These are the spiritual forces of good.

THE INVISIBLE WAR

This invisible spiritual war is real, and it involves everyone. The spiritual war is not a natural battle between flesh and blood. It is not a battle of a man against man. It is not a visible battle. It is an invisible struggle in the spirit world. It is a battle within and around a person. The reason it is not a visible war is because spirits are involved and a spirit does not have flesh and blood. Spiritual warfare is fought in different dimensions.

THREE AREAS THIS MAY OCCUR

1. A social battle that takes place between the believer and the world. (John 15:18-27 NKJV)
2. A personal battle between the flesh and the spirit. (Galations 5:16-26 NKJV)
3. A supernatural battle between believers and evil spiritual powers. (Ephesians 6:10-27 NKJV)

It is very clear using our key verse that all believers wrestle against the evil forces. Conflict from time to time happens to all of us. This war will rage until Jesus returns. The enemy of our soul, Satan, fights to maintain control of the kingdoms of the world. He continually fights God's authority. He blinds the minds of unbelievers and frequently attacks believers in the following areas that we call the 4 W's. He attacks in the area of *worship*, the *Word* of God, in their everyday *walk* in life, and in their *work* for God.

He and his demonic forces are invisible. It all began when God created an angel of light in Heaven called Lucifer, who was part of the Kingdom of God when he decided that he wanted to take over God's Kingdom. A group of angels joined with him in the rebellion against God. They were cast out of Heaven by God and formed their own kingdom on earth. (Isaiah 14:12-15 NKJV). The Bible says, "and there was war in Heaven Michael and his angels fought against the dragon (Satan); and the dragon fought and his angels. And the great dragon was cast out, the old serpent, called the Devil, which deceives the whole world he was cast out in to the earth, and his angels were cast out with him." (Revelation 12:7-9 NKJV) At that time, Lucifer became known as Satan and the rebellious angels followed him as demons. Satan directs his demonic army on assignments. To harass, to entice, and to lure into evil, wicked things.

Understanding strategies of spiritual warfare will give us the ability to deal with these evil powers. We do not have to fear them when the Holy Spirit lives inside of us. He is our defender, but we have to become rooted in the reality that the Holy Spirit is here to protect, guide and help us, and know beyond a shadow of a doubt that He is there for us. He will fight for us, but we need to be prepared for the battle, and well-grounded in the Word of God so that we do not weaken in a state of fear.

As believers in God's Army we must be grounded in the Word and have a stable prayer life. We cannot emphasize this enough. As we become strong in His word, then we know that the enemies' strategies are really directed at God, His plan, and His people. The fight is against good and evil.

We need to clearly understand who we are fighting today; it is not people. It is the spirit of this age. It is against Satan and his demonic forces, but know this, "Because He who is in you is greater that he who is in the world." (I John 4:4 NKJV) The enemy loves when believers are ignorant of his devises and strategies, because then he knows he can attack them and weaken them to the point of bringing them down.

We must be aware of Satan's strategies because the word says, "Lest Satan should take an advantage of us for we are not ignorant of his devices." (II Corinthians 2:11 NKJV) It is important that we learn all of Satan's strategies of attack. We are not to be ignorant of his devices as stated above. We cannot correct the evils of this world through education, legislation, and through an improved environment. The visible evils of this world are the results of an underlying cause. They cannot be corrected using natural means. Our political wars cannot be fought with human intellect but only by and through the power of the Holy Spirit. "Instead, God chose things the world considers foolish in order to shame those who think they are wise, and He chose things that are powerless to shame those who are powerful." (I Corinthians 1:27 NLT)

We are all born into sin. We have a sin nature when we are born into this world. The natural inclination is to do evil. (Romans 3:23 - Romans 5:12) Many people think if they just ignore Satan, he will not bother them. Nothing could be further from the truth. This is one of Satan's main strategies. He tries to cause people of the body of Christ to become immobile by his terror tactics. Have we not seen this especially since the year of 2020 to the present, evil attacks, terrorizing people, and immobilizing them with fear?

STRATEGIES IN SPIRITUAL WARFARE

In the Army of the Lord we must gain understanding of these strategies to fight and defeat Satan. These are steps to take and to be prepared for any battle we may face. Understand that we are standing in the power of the living God, and that the Blood of Jesus has already won the war, WE WIN! We know that His word is clear, "GREATER is HE that is IN us, then he that is in the world." (I John 4:4).

We emphasize this repeatedly it is highly important that we understand this. We do not war against people, "Be prepared. You're up against far more than you can handle on your own. Take all the help you can get, every weapon God has issued, so that when it's all over but the shouting you'll still be on your feet. Truth, righteousness, peace, faith, and salvation are more than words. Learn how to apply them. You'll need them throughout your life. God's Word is an indispensable weapon. In the same way, prayer is essential in this ongoing warfare. Pray hard and long. Pray for your brothers and sisters. Keep your eyes open.

Keep each other's spirits up so that no one falls behind or drops out." (Ephesians 6:13-18 MSG) Spiritual Warfare Strategies focus on the Kingdom of Satan and those things which rage against the Kingdom of God.

It is vitally important that you engage in reading the Word of God every day, and learn how to pray and engage with God and become consistent with your everyday personal walk with Him. We must build our spiritual strength up, so when we come up against the battles we will face in the Army of the Lord, we will not be afraid and will be able to stand strong. We need to know the Word of God and how to stand in the anointing we receive in spending time with Him in daily prayer.

LEARN THESE SCRIPTURES

FOCUS ON THEM IN YOUR PERSONAL TIME WITH GOD

PONDER OFTEN

"The Spirit of the Lord is upon me, because He had anointed me to proclaim good news to the poor. He has sent me to proclaim liberty to the captives and recovering sight to the blind, to set at liberty those who are oppressed." (Luke 4:18 NKJV)

We see HOW God anointed Jesus of Nazareth with the Holy Spirit and with power. "He went about doing good and healing all who were oppressed by the devil, for God was with Him." (Acts 10:38 NKJV)

We must ALL remember when we go to fight the battles that it is "Not by might, nor by power, but by My Spirit says the Lord of hosts." (Zechariah 4:6 NKJV)

Why is it important to study the Word of God? Because "the anointing that you received from Him abides IN you, and you have no need that anyone should teach you. But as His anointing teaches you about everything, and is true, and is not a lie - just as it has taught you, "ABIDE IN HIM." (I John 2:27 NKJV)

"But the Helper, the Holy Spirit, whom the Father will send in my name, He will teach you all things and bring to your remembrance all that I have said to you." (John 14:26 NKJV)

When on the field you are in the combat zone. In this day, and age, it is possible that someone would like to get into a debate with you concerning the Bible or possibly a scripture you may have just given to them. It is important to understand that this is one strategy the enemy uses. It is his dart he sends to get the conversation off course. This is a tactic he uses to try to either divert the conversation or stop it from going any further. God may give you a scripture in the middle of a conversation to say back which at times can break the 'debater", but we need to help our soldiers understand, that is not what you are there for. Do not stand and 'debate' the Word of God with anybody. You can discuss a verse but when you see it going in the direction of just being argumentative, end the conversation and thank them for their input. Move on. You have sown a good seed, let the Holy Spirit take it from there. Guard against becoming offensive in your conversation. If the person you are talking with in a conversation becomes verbally and or physically aggressive, try to remain calm, loving, but in a sweet and gentle way end the conversation, then nicely just walking away.

When sharing the gospel with someone who has never heard it, this is conducting offensive warfare. You are claiming new territory in the name of Jesus. We never want to get into an argument with the person we are trying to share the gospel with. If things begin to get very intense and even belligerent, it is best to gently end the conversation appropriately and walk away. Do not try to make a point and leave angry. That is not a good representation as a soldier of the message you have tried to relay.

This is one strategy the enemy loves to use, and that is to get people arguing over the Word.

"But avoid foolish disputes, genealogies, contentions, and strivings about the law; for they are unprofitable and useless." (Titus 3:9 NKJV) Apostle Paul cautioned us about rebellious people who were "full of empty talk and deception." (Titus 1:10 NKJV)

Timothy warned us to watch out for those who promote empty speculations rather than God's plan. "They are covered with the clouds of conceit. They are loaded with controversy, and they love to argue their opinions and split hairs. The fruit of their ministry is contention, competition, and evil suspicions." (I Timothy 6:4 TPT) In this day and age, you are bound to run into people like that. God has given us a weapon in how to handle these situations in the scriptures given above.

SURPRISE ATTACKS

Always be ready for surprise attacks. Today we face terrorism, protests, and even gang related activity, depending on the area that you occupy. The point is, the target in which the assaults are directed is often caught unawares and is unprepared. Confusion is a tactic that the enemy uses. "You are of the offspring of your father, the devil, and you serve your father very well, passionately carrying out his desires. He's been a murderer right from the start! He never stood with the truth, for he's full of nothing but lies - lying is his native tongue. He is a master of deception and the father of lies!" (John 8:44 TPT) Conflicts and rebellions have their source in Satan, both in the physical and spiritual worlds. Defeat is generally the result when caught off guard. "Stir up the anointing that is in you." (II Timothy 1:6 NKJV)

Satan also uses the methods of violent, offensive, surprise attacks. He will attack you when you least expect it, so have a plan in place in advance. Suggestions would be that if you have a security department in your church, talk with them about a plan. If you do not have a security department, then send a trustworthy person to set up a meeting with your local police chief or chief chaplain and talk with them about preparation for what you are planning to do in your city. Ask your people, chances are someone knows of a Christian Law Enforcement Officer that they can suggest you contact. But, have a plan in place. This is not meant to scare anyone, but this is meant to prepare for battle. You mean business when you are going into the enemies' territory to take it back for Christ. Be prepared! You do not have to make this public knowledge to everyone, we know angels will protect us in the spiritual realm, but we also need to be wise in the physical realm. Our world is an evil place and we must be ready for anything and everything.

In the natural world, the greatest concentration of troops is sent to specific locations and to a decisive battlefield. This should be true as well in the spirit world. This is why we are raising up and Army of the Lord. They need to be trained and ready for battle, all kinds of battles, expected and unexpected.

The Army of the Lord is a concentration of troops prepared with spiritual resources in strategic locations and is necessary for successful warfare. This is in terms to who we will be spreading the gospel.

COMMUNICATION

Communication from the pastor or leader is vital and important in both natural and spiritual warfare. The troops must be able to communicate both to receive instructions, details, and direction.

Guard against another strategy that the enemy will try to use, and that is miscommunication. He will meddle in any way he can, so it is important that the pastor or leader has someone who is always beside him to help keep those communication airways clear from distraction or any obstruction possible.

The enemy's strategy in this situation is to destroy your lines of communication. He will try to prevent you as the leader and your army from reading God's Word and praying privately, and as a group. KEEP YOUR GUARD UP! DO NOT LET THIS HAPPEN!!!! If anyone neglects these areas, it will be easy to be defeated. This is where everyone receives their spiritual power. Your Commander on the front line must constantly receive of God's instructions and encouragement through his private time of bible study and prayer.

Everyone in the army must be cooperative with one another in their effort to defeat the enemy and win souls. They must come together under the direction of their leader. They move together as a unified force and they move forward together as a unit.

Have you ever seen an army that was not in uniform? Here is why it is important that we all wear uniforms and dress the same. Here is the purpose.

UNIFORMS

No man is an island in the Army of the Lord. We are one. Therefore, it is important that everyone wears a uniform. The tradition of wearing church T-Shirts is all good, but in the Army of the Lord we wear our army uniforms. This means dark green camo pants, army dark green hats, black socks, and black shoes. These can be black tennis shoes, or some form of black shoes, or even boots. We leave this to the persons discretion. We ask that everyone's shirts be tucked in and some may desire wearing a black belt. Shirts hanging out can give a sloppy testimony. Appearance is important. We all want to look uniform and of excellence when we are out in the combat zone representing our Commander-in-Chief.

EXPLANATION

OF THE USE OF ALL BEING DRESSED IN UNIFORMS

1. Why such an emphasis on our uniforms? Because just as the national army tends to be standardized and give distinction to all those who are involved, it also indicates to on lookers that everyone in the Army of the Lord uniforms have been trained and equipped to serve.

2. This also helps to identify those who are with us, and displays to those around us that we are an organized group together. Uniform will also indicate to the public that we are an organized group of warriors. It gives everyone on the team and all leaders the capability of spotting our people when we are out in a crowd ministering as well.

3. It symbolizes a group of a trained organization.

4. Uniforms also indicate protection. People will see a coordinated group of people in harmony.

5. Also, they are not as likely to interfere with people who appear to be in a group.

6. It displays teamwork. Please note No medals or medallions of the professional military uniforms or armed services should be displayed or attached to the Army of the Lord uniforms in any way, nor at any time.

7. This will also speak to the group of the importance to work together effectively.

8. It helps to demonstrate a coordinate bond as one.

9. It displays equal in rank of importance.

10. Sends a very strong message that we are one and we have a leader or leaders that are observing our actions and behavior.

Bringing an understanding as to why we dress alike and wear uniforms helps bring understanding to its purpose. We are the Army of the Lord, and we are representing Jesus in all we do. Our actions, our reactions, language, attitudes, and approach of sharing the gospel.

This sends a message to all those who see people coming together in uniform, that something is about to transpire. Curiosity is aroused, and questions begin to come to people's minds. When the Army of the Lord conducts themselves in a godly manner, it speaks volumes to people who are around.

As a group, the troop feels unified, respected, and honors one another. It is a positive way to give immediate recognition and even honor to strangers and in your city. As you represent the Lord Jesus Christ in days ahead, you will be honored by those in your city. This will also reflect your church and ministry as well.

Be sure you give them plenty of time to purchase the uniforms. Begin announcing as soon as possible. Give people an ample amount of time so that everyone will be able to participate. Some are able to buy immediately the complete uniform quickly. Others may need time to gather their funds together. By extending time over the course of the lesson, this gives people time to save money up and purchase their outfit. We do ask that everyone purchase army green camo pants, an army green military cadet army cap. They can purchase these anywhere. Our 'Army of the Lord' T-shirts are specially designed with our "God Invasion - Releasing Revival" logo on the front left pocket area. This clearly states our purpose and mission as being one. We will post at the end of the book where the T-Shirts may be purchased for a reasonable price with us, so everyone will have the same uniforms. Having everyone dressed alike is very important for representing the Army of the Lord when you go out on into your city as a unit. Some of you will be tempted to have your own T-Shirts designed and printed locally. We ask that you contact us prior to your purchase so we can give some input in regards to everyone looking the same regardless of the city, state, nation, or country you are in. Thank you for being understanding in this area.

We want to all be dressed alike around the world so that when we go out on a mission we are easily identifiable. The uniforms help us to achieve that purpose especially when we are out in the combat zone.

HONOR ALL RANKS IN THE ARMY OF THE LORD

It is very important that we honor all levels of our Armies ranks. "And now, friends, we ask you to honor those leaders who work so hard for you, who have been given the responsibility of urging and guiding you along in your obedience. Overwhelm them with appreciation and love! Get along among yourselves, each of you doing your part. Our counsel is that you warn the freeloaders to get a move on. Gently encourage the stragglers, and reach out for the exhausted, pulling them to their feet. Be patient with each person, attentive to individual needs. And be careful that when you get on each other's nerves you don't snap at each other. Look for the best in each other, and always do your best to bring it out."

(I Thessalonians 5:12-18 MSG)

CHAPTER 6
GOD'S BATTLE STRATEGY

"And from the days of John the Baptist until now the Kingdom of Heaven suffers violence, and the violent take it by force." (Matthew 11:12 NKJV)

God has a purpose and He has a battle plan for His people. When we understand God's purpose and plan, we are not tempted to become discouraged in the conflicts in life that we may face, both in our private world and in the Army of the Lord. Understanding the purpose of God behind the battle, we will then be prepared for battle in the combat zone.

"For the word of God is living and powerful, and sharper than any two-edged sword, piercing even to the division of soul and spirit, and of the joints and the marrow, and is a discerner of the thoughts and intents of the heart." (Hebrews 4:12 NKJV) We know that the Bible says, "He who sins is of the devil, for the devil has sinned from the beginning. For this purpose, the Son of God was manifested, that he might destroy the works of the devil." (I John 3:8 NKJV) Satan battles with one ultimate goal in mind and that is to bring people into his kingdom, which is hell.

Our battle is to go out in the highways and byways and talk to people on a normal conversational level, and gently bring in the Word of God. We cannot convince anybody, we can share our story, which generally speaking can relate to people, and then bring in the Word of God. When you share your story with people, ask them if they can relate to any part of it? Once you have gained entrance into having a conversation with them, then you can add the Word of God, which will not return "void, but it shall accomplish what I please, and it shall prosper in the thing for which I sent it." (Isaiah 55:11 NKJV). God's Word will prosper. Rest in that. The person may not at the moment be ready to receive Jesus, but His Word will linger in their spirit. Rest in the fact that you have sown seed into their heart. Someone else may come along and reap what you have sown. You can rest assured that like Apostle Paul said, "I planted, Apollos watered, but God gave the increase. So then neither he who plants in anything, nor he who waters, but God who gives the increase." (I Corinthians 3:6-8 NLT)

The reason that Jesus came into the world was to destroy the works of Satan and when He did, He came into immediate opposition with the enemy. We know "The thief does not come except to steal, and to kill, and to destroy." But Jesus said, "I have come that they might have life and have it more abundantly." (John 10:10 NLT)

As believers in Christ in the Army of the Lord, be prepared to destroy the works of the devil in the hearts and minds of men and women, as well as seeing their minds set free and transformed by the mighty hand of God. Know that God's Word says He has given us authority according to Mark 16. Jesus Himself sat at the table with the disciples and literally "rebuked their unbelief" and their "hardness of heart." Why? "Because they did not believe those who had seen Him after He had risen." (Mark 16:14 NLT). A great resurrection of Jesus Christ had transpired right before their eyes, yet some still did not believe! After He rebuked them, then He said, and this applies to every believer today, "Go into all the world and preach the gospel to everyone. Anyone who believes and is baptized will be saved; but anyone who does not believe will be condemned. These signs will accompany those who believe; They will cast out demons in My name and will speak in new languages. They will be able to handle snakes with safety, and if they drink anything poisonous, it won't hurt them. They will be able to place their hands on the sick, and they will be healed." (Mark 16:15-18 NLT) "The blind see, the lame walk, the lepers are cured, the deaf hear, the dead are raised to life, and the Good News is being preached to the poor. "And he added, "God blesses those who do not fall away because of me." (Matthew 11:5-6 NLT)

The purpose in raising up an Army of the Lord and teaching and training them the battle plan of the Lord, is for them to go out and use the authority that God gave them.

God is going to use people to do great things in this end time. We need to be very careful that none of us become proud and take credit for what God does. We cannot do any of this outside of God. Know the purpose of these things is to validate the living God to the unbeliever. "And God confirmed the message by giving signs and wonders and various miracles and gifts of the Holy Spirit whenever he chose." (Hebrews 2:4 NLT).

"Most assuredly, I say to you, he who believes in Me, the works that I do He will do also; and greater works than these he will do, because I go to my Father. If you ask me anything in My name, I will do it." (John 14:14 NKJV)

"The harvest is huge. But there are not enough harvesters to bring it in. As you go, plead with the Owner of the Harvest to send out many more workers into his harvest fields. Now, off you go! I am sending you out even though you feel as vulnerable as lambs going into a pack of wolves. You won't need to take anything with you – trust in God alone. And don't get distracted from my purpose by anyone you might meet along the way." (Luke 10:2-3 TPT)

This is a cry from the heart of the Father. He is putting forth a cry for us to go out and reap the harvest of souls. He is placing the responsibility on every believer. We have a mighty task before us. We are not alone. He has promised to be with us every step of the way. Pastors, leaders, and home coaches, raise up soldiers and begin an Army of the Lord in your city. As you begin to take the step of faith and follow it by putting soldiers out on the battlefield, you will begin to see the Spirit of the Lord, come along side and give you a fresh anointing to reap a move of God in your city. Do not give up after the first attempt. Be faithful and be consistent. Go forth into your city, and reach those who are in need. God will expand your territory, and in time, you will see your community begin to change, it will flow over into your city. Spark a revival and watch the fire of God begin to burn. Train your soldiers to take back what the enemy has taken from you. "God will never be mocked! For what you plant will always be the very thing you harvest. If you plant the good seeds of Spirit-life you will reap beautiful fruits that grow from the everlasting life of the Spirit. And don't allow yourselves to be weary in planting good seeds, for the season of reaping the wonderful harvest you've planted is coming! Take advantage of every opportunity to be a blessing to others, especially to our brothers and sisters in the family of faith." (Galations 6:7-9 TPT). Everyone will be blessed who participates. You will see a plentiful harvest in every area of your ministry. Your congregation will grow into a vibrant community of believers, and the finances will be in abundance to meet every need you have. Overflow will come to you and your people in every way. Blessings will overtake you. This will be a byproduct of your people bringing in the harvest.

CHAPTER 7
EQUIPPING THE SOLDIER

"For at that time they came to David day by day to help him, until it was a great army, like the army of God." (I Chronicles 12:22 NKJV)

It is important that we understand why, what, and how we plan to move forward together in the Army of the Lord. So we will begin by answering with the "why" question.

The Philistines worshipped strange gods, opposed spiritual discipline, and were wicked people. They were always against God's people in Israel. 'Uzziah was sixteen years old when he became king, and he reigned fifty-two years in Jerusalem… he did what was right in the sight of the Lord…He sought God…had understanding in the vision of God; and as long as he sought the Lord, God made him prosper. Now he went out and made war against the Philistines…God helped him against the Philistines… Arabians… Meunites…and the Ammonites…His fame spread…" (II Chronicles 26:3-8 NKJV).

It is important for us to understand that we face similar enemies in our land, those that oppose the gospel of Jesus Christ. We can gain understanding and apply these principles to ourselves. Here we see that seeking the Lord and inquiring of Him will give "understanding" in this vision of God concerning the Army of the Lord. Like Uzziah, if we seek God, keep Him first, and follow through on the vision God has given us, God will help us to prosper. This scripture reveals to us that He will honor us too, when we do right in the sight of the Lord. Battles will be won.

Our vision of seeing God bring revival to your city, we know that this is God's heart. "Blow the trumpet in Zion, and sound the alarm in My holy mountain! Let all the inhabitants of the land tremble; For the day of the Lord is coming. For it is at hand; a day of darkness and gloominess, a day of clouds and thick darkness, Like the mourning clouds spread over the mountains". God wants us to go out and proclaim His gospel to those who are lost and dying without hope. (Joel 2:1-2 NKJV)

We believe that the Army of the Lord will be coming together all over this nation preparing and moving out to take their city and believing for all nations to join us and come together for Christ. Joel explains it like this. "A people come, great and strong, the like of whom has never been, nor will there ever be any such after them, even for many successive generations." (Joel 2:2 NKJV)

Every city, state, and nation can have revival. Every city can see souls saved and brought into the Kingdom of God. This is goal for every pastor, every leader, for the people of God! This is why we are helping you to raise up and Army of the Lord in your city. "Faith without works is dead!" The Word of God is true, it clearly says, "My dear brothers and sisters, what good is it if someone claims to have faith but demonstrates no good works to prove it? How could this kind of faith save anyone?" (James 2:14 TPT). Like David, we will see 'day by day' people join the Army of the Lord, "until it was a great army, like the army of God." (I Chronicles 12:22 NKJV).

"This is what I will do in the last days - I will pour out my Spirit on everybody and cause your sons and daughters to prophesy, and your young men will see visions, and your old men will experience dreams from God. The Holy Spirit will come upon all my servants, men and women alike, and they will prophesy. I will reveal startling signs and wonders in the sky above and mighty miracles on the earth below. Blood and fire and pillars of clouds will appear. For the sun will be turned dark and the moon blood-red before that great and awesome appearance of the day of the Lord. But everyone who calls on the name of the Lord will be saved." (Acts 2:17-21 TPT). This was also stated similarly in the book of Joel 2:28. It was said in both the Old and the New Testament that indicates this is for our day and age.

For centuries people flocked to one location when a true revival broke out. Powerful moves of God and revivals are recorded in books many have read. We understand the vital importance of a strong foundation of prayer. Prayer is the key to revival! We will be discussing the War Room in Chapter 9, in more depth concerning the importance of prayer and intercession. It is essential and must be the foundation and power that will launch your people into a deeper level with God. It will propel you forward as you have an army immersed in the power of prayer and intercession. We know and believe it's "not by might, nor by power, but by My Spirit says the Lord of hosts." (Zechariah 4:7 NKJV) Our dependency will be on the Lord Jesus Christ!

It is a new day, and God is doing a NEW thing (Isaiah 43:19). It is "not His will that any should perish". (II Peter 3:9 NKJV). He is coming back soon and the signs He forewarned us about are happening right now. They are all around us and everywhere.

"But know this, that in the last days perilous times will come; For men will be lovers of themselves, lovers of money, boasters, proud, blasphemers, disobedient to parents, unthankful, unholy, unloving, unforgiving, slanderers, without self-control, brutal, despisers of good, traitors, headstrong, haughty, lovers of pleasure rather than lovers of God, having a form of godliness but denying its power." (II Timothy 3:1-4 NKJV) We have never in our lifetime ever seen the degree of evil we are witnessing today as mentioned in this one passage alone.

The good news is found in (Joel 3:1, 9 NKJV), "For behold, in those days and at that time, when I bring back the captives of Judah and Jerusalem, I will also gather all nations… Prepare for war! Wake up the mighty men, let all the men of war draw near, let them come up." "Put in the sickle, for the harvest is ripe…the wickedness is great. Multitudes, multitudes in the valley of decision! For the day of the Lord is near in the valley of decision." (Joel 3:13-14 NKJV)

"The harvest is huge. But there are not enough harvesters to bring it in." (Luke 10:2 TPT)

In the passage in Matthew, we see that "Jesus went throughout all the cities and villages, teaching in their synagogues and proclaiming the gospel of the kingdom and healing every disease and every affliction." (Matthew 4:23 NKJV) "But when He saw the multitudes, He was moved with compassion for them, because they were weary and scattered, like sheep having no shepherd. Then He said to his disciples, "The harvest truly is plentiful, but the laborers are few. Therefore, pray the Lord of the harvest to send out laborers into the harvest." (Matthew 9: 37-38 NKJV)

This is the urgency of the hour that we raise up an Army of the Lord to begin to take back what the devil stole from us. Our cities, our towns, our states and our nations. Now more than ever we must stand on the verse, "I can do all things through Christ who strengthens me." (Philippians 4:13 NKJV)

"Therefore, be imitators of God as dear children." (Ephesians 5:1 NKJV) This means we are to "mimic" to be an "imitator" of God. This is a command for the people of God. We are to "go out into the highways and hedges and compel them to come in." (Luke 14:23 NKJV). This is our responsibility as believers in Jesus Christ to go out into our city, back allies, country roads, outside of our walls, and insistently persuade the people to come in. Why? So the house of God might be full. God wants His house FILLED!

TEAMWORK

- Team Up with Those Who Follow God - (Psalm 133:1 NKJV).
- "Alone we can do so little; together we can do so much." Helen Keller
- Look Out For One Another - (Nehemiah 4:16-17 NKJV)
- MINISTER IN TEAM EFFORT - (I Corinthians 12:14 - 25 NKJV)
- Benefits of Believers Working Together - (Philippians 2:1-5 NKJV)
- Multiplies Individual Effects - (I Peter 2:4-8 TPT).

It is important to have effective teams to complete the tasks of winning lost souls. In order to accomplish our mission there must be mutual trust in the leaders and in one another. You know who you can give responsibilities too that will follow through and carry out the tasks. This will be important in mobilizing the troops in preparation, when you coordinate and collaborate with team members for "Boots on the Ground", and when going out into the combat zone. We will learn more about this in chapter 10.

Teamwork from the time people join up, to going out with "Boots on The Ground". Teamwork is one of the most important parts of this ministry. If you do not work together as a team, you will fail. They emphasize this in the natural army, how much more must we focus on this in the Army of the Lord? To have a great team, you have to have a great leader. Teamwork is about full support of the leader and one another. Teamwork, like in the natural army, is about being ready with your weapons to take on the enemy. You must be thinking together as one. Prayer will help to unify everyone in spirit, mind, and proper alignment for the task set before them. God through His word has set the standards. This is why preparation before we go out into the enemy's territory is essential.

OFFICERS IN THE ARMY OF THE LORD

Commander-in-Chief

"No, but as Commander of the army of the Lord I have now come."

(Joshua 5:14 NKJV)

Generals - (II Chronicles 17:12-19 NLT)

Captains of 50's, 100's, 1,000's

(Numbers 31:1, I Samuel 17:18, II Kings 1:9 NKJV)

GREAT MILITARY LEADERS

Abraham – (Gen. 14)

Moses – (Exodus 17)

Joshua – (Judges 6-12)

Gideon – (Judges 6:11)

Saul – (I Samuel 11-15)

David – (I Samuel 18:30 / I Samuel 5:8 / I Samuel 18)

Asa – (II Chronicles 14)

Jehozabad – (II Chronicles 17:18)

Chapter 7　　　　　　　　　　　　　　EQUIPPING THE SOLDIER

Uzziah - (II Chronicles 26)

God establishes leaders in the Army of the Lord. They each are assigned to various tasks. You might find this helpful as you begin your Army of the Lord. As you grow, you will be able to assign various levels to achieve various tasks. We see this all throughout the Word.

CHAPTER 8
THE WAR ROOM

"But you, when you pray, go into your room, and when you have shut your door, pray to your Father who is in the secret place; and your Father who sees in secret will reward you openly." (Matthew 6:6 NKJV)

This war is real! The invisible army of the enemy is at work heavily because his time is running out. Signs of the times are everywhere. "But know this, that in the last days perilous times will come. For men will be lovers of themselves, lovers of money, boasters, proud, blasphemers, disobedient to parents, unthankful, unholy, unloving, unforgiving, slanderers, without self-control, brutal despisers of good, traitors, headstrong, haughty lovers of pleasure rather than lovers of God, having a form of godliness but denying its power, from such turn away." (II Timothy 3:1-5 NKJV) We must get this message, and understand it loud and clear. Jesus is coming back soon. We do not know when, but these scriptures are strong indications of the signs of the End Times.

We have all observed over the recent years a tremendous spiritual decline in our society. Anger, hatred, violence in the streets, murders, stealing, and the horrendous burning down of people's businesses and dreams. They all have reached a new intensity like we have never seen before. There is not a person or entity that has not in some way or another been impacted by this latest turn of events. Churches, ministries, and people all over the

Chapter 8 THE WAR ROOM

United States and all throughout the world have been praying earnestly for revival for many, many years now. We have saturated our world with prayer. The ground is prepped and ready. The seed has been sown and now it is time to bring in the spiritual harvest.

My father was a farmer and planted various types of crops, one being wheat. I watched him work the fields diligently. He would prepare the ground by plowing and overturning the dirt, disc, planted the seed, and then used a cultivator to break up small weeds and grass to prevent them from taking over the seed that was planted. He then added fertilizer into the soil, and waited and prayed for the rain, then the time came to bring in the harvest. There was great anticipation as he began to see the seed pop through the ground and grow, but when harvest time came, he did not sit back and fold his arms and wait for it to come in. He had to finish the work! When the harvest was ready, he went out and worked those fields again. He harvested the grain. I still can see in my mind the wheat pouring from the combine into the bins of the trucks that would then take it to the mill. It all was a process.

I see a parallel of that to the church and ministries today. The work has been done, but now it is time to reap the harvest. People are not coming into the churches today like they use too. In fact, too often they are reluctant to come. I have talked with people who have been in the church or ministry for years. There are a few who still want to serve in the church, but many have been burned out, and pastors and leaders are often finding it hard to find people to serve. However, in talking with many people, I find they want to do something, they just do not know what they want to do. The world is waiting for us. Though it appears they are rejecting Christians today, not everyone is. There are many who are ready to take hold of something that will bring and offer them hope.

"The harvest is huge. But there are not enough harvesters to bring it in. As you go, plead with the Owner of the Harvest to send out many more workers into his harvest fields." (Luke 10:2 TPT). It is now time to raise up an army inside your present situation, teach and train your people with a new approach. So many are ready to become involved in something new, something exciting. Pastors and leaders this is an opportunity of a lifetime. "Put in the sickle, for the harvest is ripe. Come, go down; for the winepress is full, the vats overflow - For their wickedness is great. Multitudes, multitudes in the valley of decision! For the day of the Lord is near in the valley of decision." (Joel 3:13-14 NKJV)

With so much war and devastation in our world today, how do we overcome all this evil? The task before us seems humanly impossible, we all know that "with men this is impossible, but with God all things are possible." (Matthew 19:26 NKJV). God has given us his answer in (Romans 12:21 NKJV). He says, "Do not be overcome by evil, but overcome evil with good." We know that God's heart is for lost souls. He is planning a great reaping of the harvest before He returns. "The Lord is not slack concerning His promise, as some count slackness, but is longsuffering toward us, not willing that any should perish but that all should come to repentance." (II Peter 3:9 NKJV) We have no doubt that we are in the last days. We find this in both the Old and the New Testaments where He says, "And it shall come to pass afterward that I will pour out My Spirit on all flesh." (Joel 2:28 NKJV) and "And it shall come to pass in the last days, says God, That I will pour out of My Spirit on all flesh…" (Acts 2:17 NKJV) We can go forth as an Army of the Lord, with the promise of the Father because, "This is what the Sovereign Lord says When I cleanse you from your sins, I will repopulate your cities, and the ruins will the rebuilt. The fields that used to lie empty and desolate in plain view of everyone will again be farmed. And when I bring your back, people will say, 'This former wasteland is now like the Garden of

Eden! The abandoned and ruined cities now have strong walls and are filled with people!" (Ezekiel 36:33-36 NLT)

The War Room is a vital part of bringing in the harvest. Special nights of prayer should be held weekly during the time leading up to the Army going out into the combat zone. Spiritual preparation is very important. Every pastor, leader, and soldier should have their hearts in alignment with God's heart. All sin should be repented of and a turning away from that sin when there is true repentance. We all know the verse well, found in (II Chronicles 7:14 NKJV) and can quote it from memory. "If MY PEOPLE who are CALLED by MY NAME, will HUMBLE THEMSELVES and pray and seek My face, and turn from THEIR WICKED WAYS, THEN I will hear from heaven, and I will forgive their sin and will HEAL THEIR LAND." This verse has very specific instruction given to us from God! Perhaps people do not turn from their sin because they don't know what their sin is. This is something to think about as pastors and leaders.

Focus on this in the beginning of our War Room nights of prayer. Deep, true, soul searching by every person is a mandate from heaven.

Most everyone is familiar with the movie put out a few years ago by Stephen and Alex Kendrick called "War Room". It was powerful and to this day has made a tremendous impact on thousands of people. They depicted the War Room just as the Word talks about in (Matthew 6:6 NKJV) as a private, quiet place to communicate with God. "But you, when you pray, go into your room and shut the door and pray to your Father who is in secret. And your Father who sees in secret will reward you openly." Since the movie, many have turned their closets into a War Room, a private place of prayer. It has taken the prayer life of many to a whole new level. They have found the joy of God answering their prayers. They have found that they can wield the weapon of prayer in the many battles they face in life and see the hand of God move in real life situations.

Those who are soldiers in the Army of the Lord, must have a personal War Room in their everyday lives. That War Room can be in a closet, a car during lunch, a back porch, and walk through a park, etc. Prayer is the key to this ministry, to fight this fight we are all facing, individually and corporately, as well. We are fighting demonic forces. There truly are wars in the heavenlies that are making themselves visible all around us. All we need to do is turn on the news and watch, it is evident everywhere.

The War Room is a vital key to revival in your city! This room must be set aside in your home, and church or ministry. It is not optional, but mandatory. Jesus placed a high priority on spending time early in the morning agonizing in praying. When He returned He found the disciples asleep. (Matthew 26:40 NKJV) "Then He came to the disciples and found them sleeping, and said to Peter, "What! Could you not watch with Me one hour? Watch and pray, lest you enter into temptation. The spirit indeed is willing, but the flesh is weak."

To this day too often the "flesh" finds it difficult to pray. Many churches have prayer meetings or prayer groups, and sad to say for so many ministries, they are the least attended by people in their church. More teaching is needed in ways that lovingly prod, teach, and encourage people concerning the importance and power of prayer, both for them personally, and for the whole church and ministry. Therefore, because it was a high priority with Jesus, it is also a high priority for this ministry. All pastors, leaders, and groups are required to be in the War Room prior to going out to into the combat zone.

Designate a day or evening and time, where all pastors, leaders, soldiers, and whole troops comes together for an hour of power in the War Room. The atmosphere should be one that is conducive to prayer and intercession. The music can be by your Praise and Worship Band, or a strong Christian Band that would like to be a part, and if you do not have either of these resources then you can create a playlist on YouTube, Spotify and other apps. It should start out with a theme song like, "God's Got An Army" by Carmen Licciardello. Songs we highly suggest would be, "The Battle Belongs to the Lord" by Phil Wickham and "Surrounded (Fight My Battles)" by Michael W. Smith, etc. All these songs reflect and remind us of our Commander in Chief that we worship and adore. Look at the Lyrics to God's Got an Army." This is our theme song for the Army of the Lord. Please note how powerful the words are all through this song. Therefore, we have chosen it as our theme song. This is who we are and what we represent.

GOD'S GOT AN ARMY

Not afraid to fight

Soldiers of the Cross

Children of the Light

Warrior of Righteousness

With Healing in their Hands

God's Got an Army

Marching through the Land

Let me hear your war cry… HEY….

Let me hear your war cry…HEY

We're a People

With ears to hear and hearts to respond

To spiritual needs of the nation

We're a showcase

Of what He'll do when we are strong

In Jesus, to a whole generation

The world won't be the same tomorrow

Because we are here today

The kingdom of Hell

Is gonna feel sorrow

Because our war cry is worship and praise

Gods got an Army

Not afraid to fight

Soldiers of the Cross

And children of the light

Warriors of righteousness

With healing in their hands

Gods got an Army

Marching through the Land

Let me hear your war cry …Hey…

Let me hear your war cry...Hey…

The Apostles and Prophets they are speaking forth

Flames of Revival they are burning

Like old Joshua went marching out to possess

There's no way our minds will be turning

Chapter 8 — THE WAR ROOM

There's joy in the battle so we commence

To change this nation's course

The Kingdom of God suffers violence

And the violent take it by force

(Take it by force)

Gods got an Army

Not afraid to fight

Soldiers of the Cross

Children of the light

Warriors of righteousness

With healing in their hands

Gods got an Army

Marching through the land.

Let me hear ... Hey

Let me hear .... Hey

I'm a Soldier (In the Army of the Lord)

I'm a Soldier (In the Army of the Lord)

I'm a Soldier (In the Army of the Lord)

I'm a Soldier (In the Army of the Lord)

We're not afraid to stand and fight

(We're not afraid to stand and fight)

We cast out demons left and right

(We cast out demons left and right)

We're strong in battle strong in prayer

(We're strong in battle strong in prayer)

We tell Satan get out of here

(We tell Satan get out of here)

Sound off (Jesus)

Sound off (Is Lord)

Sound off (Jesus IS Lord!)

Jesus IS LORD!

REMEMBER This song is our **theme song**, and it can be found on YouTube God's Got An Army – Carmen – Lyric video for Vacation Bible Schools (VBS).

Our music selection should represent Jesus is what we are all about. We are in a War with Him, and our songs should focus on songs as we mentioned above. This sets the atmosphere for warfare and like a pep rally to pull the troop together, so we are all one in Him. Focused on Jesus! Remind them that the battle does belong to the Lord, and we are going out representing Him. Scripture should be read as in (Deuteronomy 33:27 NKJV) that says, "The eternal God is your refuge, and underneath are the everlasting arms; He will thrust out the enemy from before you, and will say, "Destroy!"

Also, "This is the land of which I swore to give Abraham, Isaac, and Jacob, saying, "I will give it to your descendants." (Deuteronomy 34:4 NLT). We have a great heritage from the Lord and fighting his battles He goes before us.

During this time break into groups and ask them to pray for God's spiritual strategy for this day. God will be very distinct in things He shares with the body of Christ. You are soldiers and His strategy as you go out is vitally important. Be attentive to specific details that He may impart to those present. Be ready to act and obey those orders as they are vitally important in this mission.

CHAPTER 9
SPIRITUAL WARFARE

"Jesus now called the Twelve and gave them authority and power to deal with all the demons and cure diseases. He commissioned them to preach the news of God's kingdom and heal the sick. He said, "Don't load yourselves up with equipment. Keep it simple; you are the equipment."
(Luke 9:1-5 MSG)

Everything has an order. God's Word says, "Let all things be done decently and in order." (I Corinthians 14:40 NKJV). First, the natural then the spiritual. God's Word clearly says, "However, the spiritual is not first, but the natural, and afterward the spiritual." (I Corinthians 15:46 NKJV)

Before we go out to conquer our city, we must understand the nature of the enemy in the natural, each soldier must understand that God has given each one the power and authority to conquer any enemy attack in the spiritual realm. "Jesus said, I know. I saw Satan fall, a bolt of lightning out of the sky. See what I have given you? Safe passage as you walk on snakes and scorpions, and protection from every assault of the Enemy. No one can put a hand on you. All the same, the great triumph is not in your authority over evil, but in God's authority over you and presence with you. Not what you do for God but what God does for you – that's the agenda for rejoicing." (Luke 10:18-20 MSG) Soldiers will be able to go forth into the combat zone with confidence knowing they are equipped by the power of the Holy Spirit for every encounter they may face.

Our strategy is based on understanding the purposes of our warfare. We base it on our communication with our Commander-in-Chief by fasting, prayer, and the Word of God. If we do not understand our purpose and God's plan, the enemy's strategy is to take life circumstances and turn them into discouragement. This is why many Christian soldiers often fail in warfare. They do not understand the purpose of God that is behind the battle plan. We have God's purpose and we will not be defeated! "So, what do you think? With God on our side like this, how can we lose? If God didn't hesitate to put everything on the line for us, embracing our condition and exposing Himself to the worst by sending His own Son, is there anything else He wouldn't gladly and freely do for us? And who would dare tangle with God by messing with the one of God's chosen? Who would dare even to point a finger? The One who died for us, who was raised to life for us, is in the presence of God at this very moment sticking up for us. Do you think anyone is going to be able to drive a wedge between us and Christ's love for us? There is no way! Not trouble, not hard times, not hatred, not hunger, not homelessness, not bullying threats, not backstabbing, not even the worst sins listed in Scripture." (Romans 8:31-38 MSG)

Every battle that is fought whether in the natural army or the spiritual army, has always had a purpose and this is the reason the war is conducted. As we move into God's strategy and battle plan, we must understand the reason for spiritual warfare. The War Room is where we gather, pray, and intercede together as one unit. There God empowers each one and births a strategy everyone follows.

Chapter 9   SPIRITUAL WARFARE

Spiritual warfare takes place in the War Room, but it also can take place on the battlefield. However, Spiritual warfare always precedes any battle the soldier may be facing, both personally and corporately. Always remember, God is in you. (Philippians 2:13 NKJV) clearly emphasizes, "For it is God who works in you both to will and to do for His good pleasure."

He is also alongside us. "God's Spirit is right alongside helping us along. If we don't know how or what to pray, it doesn't matter. He does our praying in and for us, making prayer out of our wordless sighs, our aching groans. He knows us far better than we know ourselves, knows our pregnant condition, and keeps us present before God. That's why we can be so sure that every detail in our lives of love for God is worked into something good." (Romans 8:28 MSG). Everything that God does or even allows in our lives is done to accomplish His purpose. Therefore, God desires each soldier to "...throw yourself wholeheartedly and full-time – remember, you've been raised from the dead into God's way of doing things. Sin can't tell you how to live. After all, you're not living under the old tyranny any longer. You're living in the freedom of God." (Romans 6:13-23 MSG). "And we know that God causes everything to work together for the good of those who love God and are called according to His purpose for them." (Romans 8:28 NLT)

There is warfare in the spirit world every day. Satan fights to bring the heart, mind, spirit, and soul into loyalty to him instead of Jesus Christ. Satan has fought against the fulfillment of God's purpose since the beginning of time.

When we commit and surrender ourselves to God, we become a target of the enemy. We do not need to fear, because every battle fought God has already won. The reason God came into the world was to destroy the works of the enemy. When this happened this infuriated the enemy. Satan's battle plan is obvious, "The thief does not come except to steal, and to kill, and to destroy." We do not need to fear at all because Jesus said, "I have come that they may have life, and that they may have it more abundantly." (John 10:10 NKJV) "I am with you always, even to the end of the age." (Matthew 28:20 NKJV)

There are so many examples in the Bible where while Jesus walked here on this earth, He defeated the enemy and He destroyed and still destroys the works of the enemy.

SCRIPTURAL STRATEGIES
FOR DEFEATING THE ENEMY

We as believers look to Jesus the author and finisher of our faith. He has a battle plan to defeat the enemy in all of our lives. When we observe how He dealt with the enemy, we can learn from His strategy. His battle plan is effective, and He always defeats the enemy. We know that it is "quick, and powerful, and sharper than any two-edged sword, piercing even to the division of soul and spirit, and of joints and marrow, and is a discerner of the thoughts and intents of the heart." (Hebrews 4:12 NKJV)

We have also learned that God delegates His power and authority to those who are born-again. To those who are disciples of Christ. He has also taught us in His Word that 'prayer' is a powerful tool. It is effective and "mighty in God for pulling down strongholds." (II Corinthians 10:3-5 NKJV)

FASTING

Fasting prior to the "Boots on the Ground" is important. Many great books are written concerning fasting. For that reason, I will not elaborate on this topic. We firmly believe in fasting. It is not used to get our way, but to find God's way. There are private and public fasts. Fasting is suggested with soldiers privately because it is a personal matter between the soldier and God. We do ask that

Chapter 9 SPIRITUAL WARFARE

the pastors and leaders call a public fast and request everyone to follow. The Daniel Fast is often a one to suggest so that everyone can do this corporately, not eating meats and sweets. Of course, people who have health issues should consult with their doctor first, and all others need to apply appropriately to their individual condition.

WHILE FASTING WE NEED TO:

1. Humble ourselves "before God with fasting" (Psalm 35:13 NKJV) What David learned in this specific fast, was a direct response to his fast. He found while praying for God's protection from his enemies, that they were not his enemies. But because David had mistreated them, this was why they reacted to him the way they had.

2. "That is why the Lord says, "Turn to me now, while there is time, Give me your hearts. Come with fasting, weeping, and mourning." (Joel 2:12 NLT)

3. Seek God for revelation for oneself and for the event or battle we are about to participate in (Daniel 9:3-9 NLT)

4. "No, this is the kind of fasting I want Free those who are wrongly imprisoned; lighten the burden of those who work for you. Let the oppressed go free and remove the chains that bind people." (Isaiah 58:6 NLT)

5. "Share your food with the hungry and give shelter to the homeless. Give clothes to those who need them, and do not hide from relatives who need your help." (Isaiah 58:7 NLT)

How long the length of the fast depends on the leadership. Jesus placed a strong emphasis on fasting, as much as He did on prayer in (Matthew 6:5-18 NKJV). He explained in (Matthew 17:21 NKJV) that certain kinds of devils can be cast out by no other means. We do not over emphasize the demon world, but as born-again believers, we must not be like ostriches and stick our heads in the sand. With the condition of our world today, it has been made clear that witchcraft, devil worship, and satanism, etc., are on the rise. As believers we have the authority over every demon in hell and fasting will give an anointing to cast demons out when they surface. We have to be aware that this does exist and we do have the God given authority and power over every demon in hell. Be ready! Soldiers are equipped and do have the power to do so. Jesus' disciples asked why they were unable to cast out the devil and the essential reason was their lack of faith. "Jesus said to them," Because of your unbelief, for assuredly, I say to you, if you have faith as a mustard seed, you will say to this mountain, 'Move from here to there,' and it will move; and nothing will be impossible for you. However, this kind does not go out except by prayer and fasting." (Matthew 17:21 NKJV). Knowing the important role of fasting in obtaining and using the power, focuses special attention to our need to fast and pray.

This informs us that there is a kind of devil that requires more than usual spiritual anointing to command. Satan knows this. We as believers need not shy away from this, but take authority and do the works that Jesus did and even greater. Jesus clearly tells us "Most assuredly, I say to you, he who believes in Me, the works that I do he will do also' and greater works than these he will do, because I go to My Father. Whatever you ask in My name that I will do, that the Father may be glorified in the Son. If you ask me anything in My name, I will do it. (John 14:12 NKJV)

There is a fast that pleases God, "Cry aloud, spare not; Lift up your voice like a trumpet; Tell My people their transgression, and the house of Jacob their sins. Yet they seek Me daily, and delight to know My ways, as a nation that did righteousness, and did not forsake the ordinance of their God." (Isaiah 58: 1-2 NKJV). He says, "they delight in approaching God." He rejoices when He sees

His people willing to lay food, social media, TV, and other things aside to simply to search their hearts, spend time with Him and to seek His face. Tremendous things happen as a result of fasts, by spending quality time and just seeking and loving Him. This is important to see revival. Prayer is a Key!

He has given us, His children, the KEYS to HIS KINGDOM. Think about that. Everything we need is available and we have complete access at any time, all in the Name of JESUS!!! Let us break this down and receive clarity on how to use the Word of God to fight spiritual battles.

THE WORD OF GOD

Jesus knew the power of the Word of God. A great example was demonstrated to us when He was tempted in the wilderness. In this encounter, a major portion of our spiritual battle plan was revealed.

Satan was in a direct confrontation with Jesus. Temptation is one of his schemes with every person that walks on the earth. Some soldiers may be tempted to quit before they even begin. Will they pass the test? First, the enemy tried to get Jesus to cast Himself down from the top of the temple. It is important that we note that Satan could not cast himself down. Why? Because the power he has is limited! Don't under estimate his power, he does have it, but what he does not have is the power over Jesus! He does not force anybody to sin, but he entices them to sin. Satan will even use God's Word to back up his temptation just as he did with Jesus. But Satan misapplied it. This also is a major scheme of the enemy that soldiers need to be aware of as they are out on the battlefield. There are those that will try to use scripture out of context to confuse the soldier. Do not fall for it. Know the Word!

There are three situations where Satan tempted Jesus using his evil forces of the world, the flesh, to war against Jesus. What was Jesus' weapon? The Word of God! The Word of God is our manual for spiritual warfare. In order for the Word of God to be used effectively in spiritual warfare, you must know the Word of God. "Jesus answered and said to them, "Your mistake is that you don't know the Scriptures, and you don't know the power of God." (Matthew 22:29 NLT) The Word of God is every soldier's manual for warfare and reveals God's spiritual battle plan for every soldier.

DELGATED POWER AND AUTHORITY

This part of the battle plan is based on the soldier's power and authority over Satan and every demonic spirit, principality, and power in hell that is given to every believer, and to every soldier. "Then He called His twelve disciples together and gave them power and authority over all demons and to cure diseases. He sent them to preach the kingdom of God and to heal the sick." (Luke 9:1-2 NKJV)

Authority is different than power. A police officer is given authority because of his position he holds with the government. He wears a uniform and has a badge, which symbolizes his authority. He has carries a weapon because there are people who do not respect that authority. The weapon is his power.

The soldier's authority over the enemy comes through your position as a born-again believer given to you by Jesus Christ. Your power comes through the enablement of the Holy Spirit. (Luke 24:49 NKJV) tells us, "My Father" sends the promise that "until you be endued with power from on high," soldiers need both the power and the authority to be effective, just as police officers do. Born-again believers receive the authority when they become born-again, but they must be empowered by the Holy Spirit. The combination of these two work hand in hand. "Behold, I send the Promise of My Father upon you; but tarry in the city of Jerusalem until you are endued with power from on high." (Luke 24:49

NKJV) In (Acts1:8 NKJV) "But you shall receive power when the Holy Spirit has come upon you; and you shall be witnesses to Me in Jerusalem, and in all Judea and Samaria, and to the end of the earth."

POWER OVER THE ENEMY

The Word of God tells us that we have the power over specific purposes. Jesus made prayer a priority. How do we know this? He prayed any time of the day or night according to (Luke 6:12-13) we read, "Now it came to pass in those days that He went out to the mountain to pray, and continued all night in prayer to God." Prayer at times took priority over Him eating. "In the meantime, the disciples pressed him, "Rabbi, eat. Aren't you going to eat?" (John 4:31-32 NKJV) It also took priority over Jesus' business as well. "Jesus said, the food that keeps me going is that I do the will of the one who sent me, finishing the work He started. As you look around right now, wouldn't you say that in about four months it will be time for harvest? Well, I'm telling you to open your eyes and take a good look at what is right in from of you. These Samaritan fields are ripe. It's harvest time!" (John 4:31-32 MSG) Are we not to be imitators of Jesus according to (Ephesians 5:1-2) Apostle Paul told the children of God to be imitators of Christ. He tells us first to be followers, and that word means mimic, be an imitator of God. If Jesus fasted and Jesus was willing to lay aside eating for the purpose of going out into the field because it is harvest time, how much more should every soldier be willing to do the same?

FASTING AND PRAYER
MUST ACCOMPANY EVERY EVENT

Jesus always sets the example for believers and soldiers of the cross to follow. Before every major event in Jesus' life, He lives His lifestyle before us which sets a pattern for every soldier. He prayed before He chose His disciples, (Luke 6:12-13 NKJV), He prayed before He fed the 5,000 (Matthew 14:19-23 NKJV). There are so many examples of how prayer preceded every event Jesus did. He prayed before His first ministry tour, "While it was still night, way before dawn, He got up and went out to a secluded spot and prayed. Simon and those with Him went looking for Him. They found Him and said, "Everybody's looking for You". Jesus said, "Let's go to the rest of the villages so I can preach there also. This is why I've come. He went to their meeting places all through Galilee, preaching and throwing out the demons." (Mark 1:35-39 MSG)

God is very detailed and specific in His Word. He desires we obey and follow His direction, leading, and guidance as Commander-in-Chief. He always has purpose behind everything He says and orchestrates. Therefore, it is so important we follow His Word precisely.

HEALING THE SICK

"A leper came to Him, begging on his knees, "If you want to, you can cleanse me. Deeply moved, Jesus put out His hand, touched him, and said, 'I want to, be clean'. Then and there the leprosy was gone, his skin smooth and healthy." (Mark 1:40-45 MSG) "For we do not have a High Priest who cannot sympathize with our weaknesses, but was in all points tempted as we are, yet without sin." (Hebrews 4:15 NKJV). As soldiers go out into the battlefield, there will be times when the battle will be, someone who is fighting sickness and disease. Our weapon is in the power we have been given. "These are some of the signs that will accompany the believers They will throw out demons in my name, they will speak in new tongues, they will take snakes in their hands, they will drink poison and not be hurt, they will lay hands on the sick and make them well." (Mark 16:17-18 MSG)

The weapon against sickness and disease is given to every soldier. We will be experiencing miracles, signs, and wonders as we go out representing the name of Jesus. There are many people out there today who simply will not believe unless they see. Doubting Thomases are everywhere, so it is not unlikely that you will not come across one. God will heal people like this to validate that He is alive and well. It is not to be used to bring glory to oneself, but to bring glory and praise to Jesus! It is important to pray prior to the troops going out to minister, ask God to lead you to those He desires to reveal Himself to in a special way, then trust and know that He will do this.

CHAPTER 10
MOBILIZING THE ARMY OF THE LORD

"The weapons of our warfare are not carnal but mighty in God for pulling down strongholds, casting down arguments and every high thing that exalts itself against the knowledge of God..." (II Corinthians 10:4-5 NKJV)

Soldiers must be aware that challenges will come as they go forth because they are going out into the combat zone. Soldiers must be trained and sharp in the wisdom of God as they go forth. This book is training material to help every leader train their soldiers so when they go out, the Holy Spirit accompanies them, because He is IN them.

When on the battlefield of the enemy he will try to derail in various ways. Sometimes during a conversation, or maybe through distractions, there may be conversational challenges. God specifically makes us aware in this verse above, that all soldiers have the aid of the Holy Spirit and God has given a weapon to every soldier. These weapons are not physical so that they do not have the nature of flesh. These weapons are invisible, spiritual weapons. They are powerful weapons; they have the power against strong arguments and reasoning's when someone tries to challenge and or reason to start a dispute. They endeavor to do this to strengthen their challenged opinion. This is why it is so important to know the Word of God!!! "NO WEAPON formed against you will prosper." (Isaiah 54:17 NKJV). "Fight the good fight of the faith." (I Timothy 6:12 NKJV) So that one day you will be able to stand before the Commander-in-Chief and say, "I have fought the good fight, I have finished the race, I have kept the faith." (II Timothy 4:7 NKJV) and stand before Him and receive the promised crown.

To mobilize the troops in the natural army is to put in the state of readiness for active military service. This stands true for the Army of the Lord as well. Our troops are being educated into the state of readiness. In this process, the soldiers of the Lord are being deployed as part of the spiritual forces.

DEFENSIVE WARFARE

The Word of God also reveals that there are two types of warfare in the natural world. It teaches us that there are both defensive and offensive spiritual strategies. Every soldier must learn to fight in both of these areas. In defensive warfare they wait and are ready when the enemy strikes, here they pull forces together to respond. When two soldiers are together, they aid one another, one may think of a scripture and the other may simplify to the hearer what that word means, or vice versa. In this type of warfare, the soldier responds to his adversary as Jesus responded to Peter. "You are seeing things merely from a human point of view, not from God's...and he turned and said to Peter, "Get behind me, Satan! You are a hindrance to me." (Matthew 16:23 TPT). Every soldier must learn to recognize the enemy in disguise. Remember, the enemy may speak through an individual, but it is not that person, it is the spirit of the enemy using that person. their decisions are forced on him by the attacker. The soldier must learn and understand in this area, they defend territory that has already been claimed. They must be ready to defend using the Word of God.

OFFENSIVE WARFARE

When in offensive warfare the soldiers are in advancing combat. This type of warfare takes the initiative to attack, not the person, but the spirit. The enemy is detected, his strategy exposed, and the soldier takes an aggressive approach against the enemy's plot. How? By using scripture that fits the situation appropriately. If none comes to mind, quickly send up a spiritual flare by silently praying and ask for God's wisdom. Using God's Word is the weapon, and it is tremendously effective. It always accomplishes God's desired intention for that specific situation. The purpose is to move in by taking this action and secure the territory. The soldiers must be attentive and sharp, must always be alert, and take the authority that has been given to them to advance the Kingdom of God. Discernment is a vital component in recognizing the tactics and strategies of the enemy.

Pastors and leaders, activating your people in spiritual warfare and training them how to reach people with the gospel is vital. Our nation is crumbling before our eyes. We are in a spirit war, evil against good. We have the answer to the problem, but it is going to take all of us working together to win this spiritual war. No one person can win this battle. Together we can make a difference! It is extremely important for pastors and ministry leaders to teach, instruct, train, and motivate people in their congregation, para-church ministries, and home groups to not sit back anymore. We can no longer watch confessing believers remain comfortable sitting on their padded chairs, coming into services week in and week out with no attempt during the week to reach their coworkers or people in the marketplace. The majority of people in your congregation do no know how to win someone to the Lord Jesus

Christ. They do not even know where to begin. To re-emphasize they need to be taught, trained, encouraged, and motivated by their pastors and leaders. Go into this knowing that people may respond rather nonchalantly in the beginning, but their interest will build as you fervently and consistently encourage and prepare them. The Army of the Lord must be trained how to advance fearlessly and courageously in the enemy's territory. It is an ageless war between light and darkness, between Satan and his demonic influences. When a light is turned on in a dark room the light breaks through the darkness, where there is no light, darkness remains. Our soldiers must carry God's light into a world that is spiritual darkness.

God's children have power and authority they need to utilize. It is every believer's responsibility to "Go into the all the world and preach the Good News to everyone." (Mark 16:15 NLT).

(Proverbs 10:5 TPT) makes it very clear, "KNOW the IMPORTANCE of a season you're in and a wise son you will be." The footnote in TPT Bible says, "To gather in the summer is to be a wise son, but to sleep through the harvest is a disgrace." The harvest time is here. It is time! It appears that the Second Coming of Jesus Christ is on the horizon. We have a much work to do. The pastor and leader cannot do this work alone, it will take an Army of the Lord working together as one unit to bring in the harvest. The time is now!

We need to consistently continue in prayer, because prayer is the key that unlocks the door to revival. We must also remember that "Faith without works is DEAD!" The Message Bible states this well, "Dear friends, do you think you'll get anywhere in this if you learn all the right words but never do anything? Does merely talking about faith indicate that a person really has it? For instance, you come upon an old friend dressed in rags and half-starved and say, "Good morning, friend! Be clothed in Christ! Be filled with the Holy Spirit!" and walk off without providing so much as a coat or a cup of soup – where does that get you? Isn't it obvious that God-talk without God-acts is outrageous nonsense? I can already hear one of you agreeing by saying, "Sounds good. You take care of the faith department; I'll handle the works department." Not so fast. You can no more show me your works apart from your faith than I can show you my faith apart from my works. Faith and works, works and faith, fit together hand in glove. Do I hear you professing to believe in the one and only God, but then observe you complacently sitting back as if you had done something wonderful? That's just great. Demons do that, but what good does it do them? Use you heads! Do you suppose for a minute that you can cut faith and works in two and not end up with a corpse on your hands? Wasn't our ancestor Abraham "made right with God by works" when he placed his son Isaac on the sacrificial altar? Isn't it obvious that faith and works are yoked partners, that faith expresses itself in works? That the works are "works of faith"? The full meaning of "believe" in the scripture sentence, "Abraham believed God and was set right with God," includes his action. It's that weave of believing and acting that got Abraham named "God's friend." Is it not evident that a person is made right with God not by a barren faith but by faith fruitful in works?" (James 2:14-24 MSG) This is a very serious matter with God.

Therefore, we all must work together to build an Army of the Lord all across the land and join hands to win our communities, cities, states, and nations back to God. It is going to take a concentrated effort of pastors and leaders catching the vision to win the lost and start a revival in your city! It is not impossible. Even lay people can form their own Army of the Lord and raise up people to start a revival in their city!

There is an urgency in the hour. We all can see the desperate need that our cities and nations are in. Believers, if we come together and rise up and grab hold of the sickle, we can begin reaping the harvest together.

We need to get rid of the old mindset of everyone flocking to just 'my church' or 'my ministry' in a revival. Your church or ministry belongs to God. The old thing is past, and God is no longer going to do it the old way as stated in Isaiah 43:18-19. When we think in this manner, we are putting limitations on God. That reveals a wrong attitude in the heart when we are demanding God to do it the way we want Him to do it. He has a much bigger picture. He sees millions of people that have been praying for decades for revival. He has heard their cry. It is His heart's desire to move in a massive revival, but we cannot put demands on Him as to how to do it. As He said, He is doing a "NEW THING and NOW it is springing forth.". He says, "For My thoughts are not your thoughts, nor are your ways My ways, says the Lord. For as the heavens are higher than the earth, so are My ways higher than your ways, and My thoughts higher than your thoughts." (Isaiah 55:8-9 NKJV) His ways are higher than our ways!

We believe as you pray, teach and train, raise up an Army of the Lord, and consistently work together, you will see God ignite a revival in your city. Multitudes of people will be won to the Lord and your ministry will overflow with the lost coming to the saving knowledge of the Lord Jesus Christ. As you begin to explode in this move of God, get outside of your box in your old way of thinking and join hands with another ministry, give them a copy of this book, so they too will raise up an Army of the Lord. Let's watch God form troops across the land, flowing over in other communities, cities, states, and nations. We all will observe as God breathes on the coals of revival fire, and this authentic move of God spreads across the land.

Look in His eyes, He wants souls to come into His Kingdom, but we need an Army of the Lord to reach the multitudes. We have work to do! We can no longer sit back with our arms folded across our chest and pray for revival. START A REVIVAL IN YOUR CITY by raising up an ARMY OF THE LORD!!!! Take your city for Christ! Start with your community, it will spread. When the fire of God begins to burn in your people, in your community, it will spread like wildfire! Your houses will be full! I believe that you will have to put up tents, and even build more to accommodate the harvest that the Lord desires to bring into His Kingdom through your city. Pray. Believe. Teach and Train. Raise up an Army of the Lord. Work together. Take over your community!!! Start a Revival in YOUR CITY!

As we come and work together, each starting a revival in our own cities, we will see a move of God like we have never witnessed before, and together we will conquer the enemy's territory. The time is now to roll up our sleeves, march in an Army of the Lord Troop, and take back what the devil has stolen from us.

Gideon overheard a man telling his friend about a dream he had. He said, "I had a dream; a loaf of barley bread tumbled into the Midianite camp. It came to the tent and hit it so hard it collapsed. The tent fell!" His friend said, "This has to be the sword of Gideon son of Joash, the Israelite! God has turned Midian - the whole camp! – over to him." When Gideon heard the telling of the dream and its interpretation, he dropped to his knees before God in prayer. Then he went back to the Israelite camp and said, "Get up and get going! God has given us the Midianite army!" (Judges 7:1-16 NLT). He goes on to say that Gideon gave very specific orders and he told them that "when I get to the edge of the camp, do exactly what I do. When I and those with me blow the trumpets, you also, all around the camp, blow your trumpets and shout, "For God and for Gideon!" They obeyed Gideons instructions and won a mighty battle.

They *rallied together, they heard from the Lord*, God appointed Gideon, and *together they won a mighty battle.* It is also to be noted, that if you read the beginning of the Chapter in Judges 7 that "God said to Gideon, "You have too large an army with you. I can't turn Midian over to them like this - they'll take credit, saying, "I did it all myself,' and forget about me. Make a public announcement "Anyone afraid, anyone who has any qualms at all, may leave Mount Gilead now and go home." Did you know that twenty-two companies headed for home, and only ten companies were left? God told Gideon, "There are still too many. Take them down to the stream and I'll make a final cut. When I say, "This one goes with you, he'll go. When I say, 'This one doesn't go, "he won't go" so Gideon took the troops down to the stream. "Do you recall the story? "God said to Gideon "Everyone who laps with his tongue, the way a dog laps, set on one side. And everyone who kneels to drink, drinking with his face to the water, set to the other side. "Three hundred lapped with their tongues from their cupped hands. All the rest knelt to drink." Then God said to Gideon, "I'll use the three hundred men who lapped at the stream to save you and give Midian into your hands. All the rest may go home." Now you know the rest of the story. You can read this in (Joshua 7 MSG).

Know this moving forward. Like Gideon, you will not get a 100% of your church to follow. That is ok. There may be some that have health issues, or age would prevent them from coming and participating, but you could give them specific things to be praying for. This would let them know they are an important part of the team even if they are unable to go out on the physical battlefield with the Army of the Lord. They can go to battle on their knees and fight the principalities and powers and help clear the way before you.

CHAPTER 11

GOD'S STRATEGY FOR AN ABUNDANT HARVEST

"Also, I heard the voice of the Lord, saying "Whom shall I send, and who will go for Us? Then I said," Here am I! Send me." (Isaiah 6:8 NKJV)

Isaiah's response was, who will volunteer for service? Today, the Lord is asking the same question. "Whom shall I send, and who will go for Us?" The Lord had a message to deliver to the nation of Judah. In verse eight He expresses His desire for a messenger. Isaiah felt his own unworthiness and became broken when he became aware of his sin. He said, "Doom! It's Doomsday! I'm as good as dead! Every word I have spoken is tainted – blasphemous even! And the people I live with are the same way, using words that corrupt and desecrate. And here I've looked in God's face! The King! God-of-the-Angel-Armies! Then one of the angel-seraphs flew to me. He held a live coal that he had taken with tongs form the altar. He touched my mouth with the coal and said, "Look. This coal has touched your lips. Gone your guilt, your sins wiped out." At this point, Isaiah was cleansed. His sin was wiped away. He was humbled and broken before the Lord. This is when the Master said, "Whom shall I send? Who will go for us?" Isaiah spoke up and said, "I'll go, send me." The very next thing that God said to him was, "Go and tell this people." (Isaiah 6:1-8 MSG) Go in knowing that there will be some people who are going to be hardheaded, they are going to act like they don't want to hear, they will appear that they don't want to see you. (Matthew 13:15 TPT) states it like this, "their minds are dull and slow to perceive; their ears are plugged and are hard of hearing, and they have deliberately shut their eyes to the truth. Otherwise, they would open their eyes to see, ad open their ears to hear, and open their minds to understand. Then they would turn to Me and I would instantly heal them."

You will also confront people like this. Do not be discouraged. Do not stop telling people, for many you will be planting a seed, and someone else will come along and water that seed, but it is the Lord that brings the increase. (I Corinthians 3:6 NKJV).

There will be those that will be open to hear what you have to say. Your soldiers will grow through the negatives and the positives. You will reap what you sow. Sometimes you may go for a while without reaping any harvest, but it is amazing how God watches your work and efforts. There *will be times* when some you witnessed to, told you they would come to your church (or ministry), then don't show up. Do not get discouraged. This is another plot in the enemy's strategy to stop your soldiers from going any further. Do not yield to the discouragement. This is part of the enemy's effort and plan. Be wise to it! God watches and is faithful. He will send other new people in their place. God sees to it that your work is rewarded and is never in vain. "So, let's not allow ourselves to get fatigued doing good. At the right time we will harvest a good crop if we don't give up or quit." (Galations 6:9 MSG)

God has a Biblical Strategy for the spiritual harvest. No doubt, you and some of your people have been sowing for some time now, for some it has been months, other's years, and others for decades and decades, perhaps you have even shed many tears in prayer. Good news! The harvest is ready, and the time is now! You can rest assured that the Word of God tells us that "They that sow in tears shall reap in joy". We pray now, God, do it again, bring rains to our drought-stricken lives so those who planted their crops in despair will shout "Yes!" at the harvest, so those who went off with heavy hearts will come home laughing, with armloads of blessing." (Psalm 126:5-6 MSG)

When we use God's Biblical Strategies, we will reap a bountiful harvest. God has spiritual strategies for the coming revival. His strategies are biblical principles that when we apply them we can be assured His way always works. He desires souls to come into the harvest. This is His hearts cry. This is God's dream! God's vision! He will give us the tools, grace, and wisdom to bring the harvest in. Not our methods, not our ways, not our plans, but His!

This revival is about souls coming into the Kingdom of God yes, and it is also about people crying out to God from their hearts. Revival must start in your church or ministry. There will have to be some deep soul searching, and preaching and teaching to help the believers to understand what sin is. How can people repent if they do not know what sin is? "If MY PEOPLE who are called by MY NAME *will humble themselves* and pray," (II Chronicles 7:14 NKJV) (that right there is a starting point). Do you know that there are people in your congregation, ministry, or home group, who really do not know how to pray? As leaders we wonder why people do not come to our prayer nights or prayer meetings. Many do not want to come for various reasons such as, they don't believe prayers really get answered, or their prayers haven't been answered, so why pray? They do not know that there are hindrances to prayer. They do not even know how to pray effectively. So, some may have doubt, and others are not sure about it, and then some prayed and didn't get the answer they were hoping for, so they gave up. We need to remember that currently, there are people coming to our services that have not been raised in a Christian home. They haven't been taught these fundamentals in their home, nor have many even been exposed to them. If the disciples asked Jesus, "Lord, teach us to pray," (Luke 11:1 NKJV) then what about those people you are responsible for that are under your care and spiritual guidance? We cannot assume all people know how to pray, when a large percentage do not. Teach them and reach them pastors and leaders. If there are people who have been in your church or ministry a long time whom you have taught, then I am sure they need a refresher course by now. If there is not a strong vein of prayer running through your church or ministry, then it is not too likely you will see a revival flow through your city. If your ministry has people who have been coming a long time, who have been taught on prayer, keep your ministry moving forward, continue with raising up your Army of the Lord. We suggest you appoint a strong warrior to teach the newcomers and babes in Christ 'how to pray'. Karyl Gaehring's book entitled "Prayer Power" is available on Amazon and is a great, simple starting point. There must be a good, solid core group of prayer and intercessors in your church and or ministry. Pastors and leaders, you must set the example and model this to your people! Witnessing is very important, but so is prayer. Jesus Himself said, "My House shall be called a 'House of Prayer" (Matthew 21:13 NKJV) This was a priority to Jesus. He demonstrated to us all throughout His Word. We see He went early in the morning to the garden to pray. When He asked His disciples, "Could you not pray with Me for 1 hour, I believe He was stating how important this one hour of prayer was.

We emphasize the importance of having a time set aside just for prayer in you church or ministry. Be consistent with it, create an atmosphere where people want to come and be a part. Worship music playing in the background is a powerful way to create this type of setting. Have it playing long before people walk in, don't be running to the sound booth to quickly turn on any song. As the pastor or leader, pray first and ask the Holy Spirit what type of atmosphere God would like to set. Pick the songs out prior to your meeting. Create a playlist so the songs can play from one to another consecutively, where it builds, and people can engage in the presence of the Lord. Have about a 90-minute play list so you can have songs playing 10 or 15 minutes before people start coming in. Let that atmosphere draw people into the presence of God. Choose songs that help people focus on God. Songs that will cause them think, reflect, and pray what the lyrics are saying in each song. They need to get their minds off their day and be able apply them to their own personal lives and situations during the prayer time. Song ideas might be "Search My Heart, O God", "This Is How I Fight My Battle", "The Healer", "Goodness of God", "Have It All", "We Will Not Be Shaken", etc. These are just to name a few to give the idea. There are so many to choose from, but they need to help people connect to God, to worship Him, and remind them He is their answer for every need they have and focus on Him.

There are various ways to guide the evening in prayer. You can hand out sheets of paper and ask them to write down what they are sensing about your city. What are some specific things they feel should be prayed over and lifted to God. When they are finished, have them lay the requests on the altar. During the personal soul-searching time, read a focus scripture, example, "Come back to me and really mean it! Come fasting and weeping, sorry for your sins! Change your life, not just your clothes. Come back to God, your God. And here's why, "God is kind and merciful". (Joel 2:12-13 MSG) Take time for every person to do some deep soul searching and be honest before God.

Chapter 11 — God's Strategy For An Abundant Harvest

Maybe some have not been concerned about the spiritual harvest. Others may want to repent for their lack of prayer, and even from their inconsistency in spending time alone with God on a personal level. There needs to be a time where they ask God to reveal to each one what has blocked or hindered their personal prayers? This time is between them alone and God.

If you are a pastor or leader and your church and or ministry has not been reaping a spiritual harvest, then we suggest the following:

- Call your whole church to come to a very important meeting
- Come together with prayer and fasting
- Take quality time to repent of specifics
- If people feel to come and repent before God and to the body of Christ, encourage that, as a leader stands beside them, and guides the process biblically
- Pray together and ask God to give us all a vision of an abundant harvest
- Unite in purpose together to fulfill the vision

One very important thing to stress is, **_if there are not enough laborers, then the harvest will rot._** I was raised on a farm during my childhood, and we had an apple orchard. Abundance of apples every year were visible to everyone. That season did not last forever. When the apples were ripe, they had to be picked. If we didn't have enough help, then the apples would get too ripe, and the stem would break away eventually from the branch and drop to the ground. If they weren't picked up and put in a bushel basket quickly, they would lay there and rot. This example also applies to the harvest of souls and is an important lesson to every believer.

If there are few laborers in the harvest field, there will be little harvest. The more workers to bring in the harvest, the more plentiful the harvest will be. If there are not enough harvesters, then the harvest will rot. When the fields are ready for the harvest, the farmer has to go out at that time. He cannot wait to hope the harvest will come in on its own without any effort. The farmer and his workers must go out and bring in the harvest.

The harvest field right now is plentiful. Pray for God to raise up people in your church and ministry who will be willing to go out and bring in the harvest.

Haggai in verse 19 says, "I am giving you a promise now while the seed is still in the barn. You have not yet harvested your grain, and your grapevines, fig trees, pomegranates, and olive trees have not yet produced their crops. But from this day onward I will bless you." (Haggai 2:19 NLT)

You may already have a good solid foundation. Perhaps you have been preparing your people and they have the anticipation of seeing a revival in your ministry, and in your city. The Holy Spirit can use you to turn the average attender into powerhouses for Jesus.

Jesus provides a spiritual blueprint and sets the example for us to model. He took fishermen, tax collectors, average people and walked with them, talked with them, and taught them the importance of reproducing Christians. His disciples had the reputation of "turning their world upside down." We find that when Paul and Silas came to Thessalonica proclaiming Jesus as King, this was said about them, "These who have turned the world upside down have come here too." (Acts 17:6 NKJV)

Think of the joy that will fill your church and city, when you begin to turn your world upside down for Jesus. Those who participate will catch the vision quickly the first time they go out together as the Army of the Lord to reap the harvest that is coming to your city!

Chapter 11　　　　　　　　　　　God's Strategy For An Abundant Harvest

In the natural world, you have sown the seed and you have been preparing for the crop. It is a principle of God that if you sow, you will reap. "This most generous God who gives seed to the farmer that becomes bread for your meals is more than extravagant with you. He gave you something you can then give away, which grows into full-formed lives, robust in God, wealthy in every way, so that you can be generous in every way, producing with us great praise to God." (II Corinthians 9:11 MSG). Every soldier needs to go out into the combat zone and help save lives for the Kingdom of God. Soldiers are willing vessels, willing to pour out of themselves at any cost. "But this I say He who sows sparingly will also reap sparingly, and he who sows bountifully will also reap bountifully." (II Corinthians 9:6 NKJV) Sowing is a principle in God's Word. Pastor and leaders, you have sown bountifully and now your harvest is here. You need to help them, by teaching and training them concerning how to bring in the harvest. You have before you a group of people who you will find, many of them are ready to do something fresh and something new. These are the soldiers you begin with to recruit. It will grow. Teach them to reproduce themselves. In other words, when they catch the vision and get excited about what God is doing, encourage them to recruit others and reproduce themselves. Then rally the troops to go out into the field and win victory after victory! Joy explodes when this happens.

Timing is important when the harvest is ready to reap. We are in an exciting time. For centuries believers have sown their lives into the harvest fields. We do not know when the Lord is returning, but there are many signs that He has told us about in His Word that are clearly pointing to His return soon. As we near His return all those who have sown and gone on before us, we have the joy of bringing a great harvest in all the nations of the world.

This is something that everyone can be involved in. Many pastors and leaders are weary. Many have tried everything they can think of to get their people back, to reach new people coming into the area. For many it is working, but not as fast as they would like to see it transpire. There are also pastors and leaders who never have been able to see their churches grow. They have tried everything. This is a God given opportunity to teach your people how to multiply and become tremendous soul winners and expand your ministry.

"So, let's not allow ourselves to get fatigued doing good. At the right time we will harvest a good crop if we don't give up or quit." (Galatians 6:9 MSG) If you have been and are faithful God has promised you will reap the harvest. Expand your tent pegs, teach and train your people to rise as a mighty Army of the Lord. Has the Word of God not told us from the beginning to "be fruitful and multiply?" (Genesis 1:28a NKJV) Do not become weary in what He has called you to do. Have you spread yourself to thin? Have you carried the load alone too long? Are you at the brink of giving everything up? Don't! Raise up an Army of the Lord in your congregation, in your ministry with the people that God has entrusted to you in your home group. Remember the word, "...unless a grain of wheat falls into the ground and dies, it remains alone; but if it dies, it produces much grain." (John 12:24 NKJV) Maybe this is where some of you are at right this moment. Has everything you poured yourself into died? Does it look like it is all over and there is no hope? Raise up an Army of the Lord! You may only have a few people left, but raise them up. Sign them up and recruit them into the Army of the Lord. Tell them, we are going to join hands together and we are going to be a powerful troop of soldiers for Lord and as an Army of the Lord, we are going to go out together and begin to bring in the harvest that is waiting for us. "Take this most seriously; a yes on earth is yes in heaven; a no on earth is no in heaven. What you say to one another

| Chapter 11 | God's Strategy For An Abundant Harvest |

is eternal. I mean this. When two of you get together on anything at all on earth and make a prayer of it, my Father in heaven goes into action. And when two or three of you are together because of Me, you can be sure that I'll be there." (Matthew 18:19-20 MSG) There is power in numbers. As you grow together, you will see the vision of God grow too. You can raise up an Army of the Lord with a small group, or with a mega church, either way, raise up and Army of the Lord to bring in the Harvest. Revival will come. "If you are faithful in little things, you will be faithful in large ones". (Luke 16:10 NLT)

Understanding and *applying* these strategies will result in abundant spiritual harvest. Together you will bring them in, it is a multiplication principle. Just as with a seed, each seed is capable of reproduction. Sowing is absolutely necessary in order to reap. The harvest does not come in the same season you sow it. You sow regardless. Many of you have continued to sow and sow. You will reap the harvest if you are faithful. You have a troop in front of you. Be it 2 or 3 or 100, or 1,000. They are soldiers for Christ. In this book you are given the keys to raising up an Army of the Lord regardless of the size of your church, ministry, or home group. They are waiting for something new, something fresh, new direction, and a new challenge.

When you raise up an Army of the Lord you will find that they will learn how to win a soul, how to spot someone who needs the encouragement, and how to lead a person to the Lord. Nothing ignites a person more than leading someone to the Lord. When you train your soldiers to fight in this spiritual battle, and they begin to see God answer their prayers, and use them in helping to build the Kingdom of God, every person represents a hot coal. When the wind of the Holy Spirit blows on that one hot coal, a fire begins to simmer, soon it bursts into flames. Another person catches the vision and wants to be a soldier in the Army of the Lord. Before you know it, they are dressed for battle and go out as a troop and begin to win your community. As your community begins to catch this fire or revival, fire spreads, and soon it will burn throughout your whole city. When this happens, you will see that you have been used of God to Start A Revival in Your City!

CHAPTER 12
BOOTS ON THE GROUND

"This is my command - be strong and courageous! Do not be afraid or discouraged. For the Lord your God is with you wherever you go." (Joshua 1:9 NLT)

MOBILIZATION

When you begin to mobilize your troops this means that you are putting them in the state of readiness for active military service. This is the process of being deployed as part of the spiritual forces of the Army of the Lord. God's spiritual strategy is now being implemented.

It is quite normal for the average believer to be a little nervous when going out for their first time. The advantage here is they are not going alone they are going with an army, a trained group of believers just like they are. We go out as a group and then break up into two's. We never want to make anyone we are approaching feel overwhelmed. So we recommend going as a team but breaking up in two's to witness.

It is so important that we know how to reach every generation. Each person has their own unique way of communicating with one another. So, it is vitally important that each soldier understands and knows how to be effective when they approach someone to share a life changing opportunity with them. The approach and first impression with individuals are very important. We do not want to be churchy, preachy, or pious at all. We want to be real! As church people, we do not always realize we have our own terminology and even phrases. We need to be careful when we are talking with unsaved and unchurched people that we do not use 'church talk' that does not relate to the unbeliever, and we do not want to come across as being fake. Be REAL! Talk like you would to your friends. Be genuine and be sincere. Be sure you don't come across as being self-righteous or 'better than' them…. Be gentle. Be kind. Do not be over bearing.

When people see a group coming dressed in army fatigues their curiosity is aroused immediately. It is different than wearing a church T-Shirt. Please do not misunderstand, there is nothing wrong with wearing a church T-Shirt. It's just people become naturally inquisitive when they see people dressed in army fatigues approaching, and wonder what is going on? Immediately you have their interest. We are just taking a new approach to reach the lost.

There are numerous ways to open a conversation with a stranger, so we will illustrate a couple of conversation starters and options of how you can reach those in your community. These are just ideas and a few ways that will encourage those in your army to be innovative in their approach to win the lost.

Soldiers need to be aware and alert. When interacting with people in our society today, lost and unsaved people are not interested in theological questions and debates. If you go out and ask people today if they would like to have a theological discussion with you, more than likely, people will walk away completely uninterested in what you have to say. We suggest this approach "Would you agree with me that life has been hard? It has been a rough couple of years, right? How has that affected you? This is being relevant. People's crisis will open them up to a conversation about God. This is a good place to start a conversation with anybody. Though we are in a spiritual war we still need to be down to earth with our approach. We need to reach each generation with the gospel of Jesus Christ in a relevant way. Sin is rampant and causing our world to spin out of control in a downward spiral. Our world is completely clueless as to what 'sin' even is, much less the consequences, damage, and havoc it can cause. The Army of the Lord must be ready to address this, in order to help people understand the horrific effects of sin.

For a couple of decades now masses came into the church with the method of fog machines being used on stage, flashing lights swirling, colorful digital screens, and praise and worship bands that gave the appearance of a concert on the stage. Pastors used, and some still use this method to attract the unsaved and unchurched. Though this worked for a decade or more and grew mega churches this method seems to be dying down to some degree. People are getting tired of performance-based churches. The fact is, without God's presence it is just another concert with a religious motivational speaker and sermon attached. The season where people flocked to this kind of church has appeared to slow down, and especially after Covid many that use to attend this type of atmosphere began looking elsewhere or shopped other churches online. God is doing a 'new thing' and we must be open to what He is desiring to do to usher in His presence in a fresh and new way.

The presence of God attracts and draws, and if there is lack of this in any church, the church will struggle to bounce back. People are looking for REAL. They are tired of the facade. We cannot stress this enough that people today are looking for what is REAL!

People today are spending hours a day looking at this small screen on their cell phones. Every day. All day! The world has figured out how to lure people using the small screen device into such areas as pornography, product pushers make us think we need a product, and the politicians use it to push their agenda. The church needs to re-evaluate what people hold in their hand every day and raise up an Army of the Lord in the technical field to reach the lost.

GENERATION Z AND MILLENNIAL ARSENAL

While researching the Gen Z generation you may be interested in reading this article in a Christian Magazine called "Faithwire." The article was written by Billy Hallowell an Editor. He interviewed a man whose name is Sean Dunn. He has a ministry called "GROUNDWIRE" and Sean is the president. Sean attributes bringing nearly <u>one hundred and ninety thousand plus</u> millennials and GenZer's to the Lord in 2021.

Sean Dunn was interviewed because of an interest in finding his way of successfully winning this generation to the Lord. He said, "his success is rooted in targeting the right people. The GenZer's look at their phones over 100 times a day." He says, "that some may look at this as a problem, but we as pastors and leaders believe that God's a real being. Even though they believe God exists they tend to ignore Him, especially in today's chaotic culture." His ministry focuses on helping young people enter a personal relationship with Christ, and he uses "popular media channels in the digital spaces through which they currently engage." He does not focus them on believing whether God is real or not, they just "remind them that He is relevant, and He becomes relevant when He intersects at that point of need in their life."

They use social media platforms to meet young people where they are. They have found that this approach has been incredibly effective. They know that they cannot get them to come to church, and they can't seem to put their phones down, so they use

Hollywood produced content. With short attention spans, Dunn said his, "organization appeals to young people with short video pieces that effectively grab their interest. Once their attention is snagged, GROUNDWIRE has people ready to chat with them 24 hours a day." (SOURCE This article was taken from Charisma News and the title of the Article is "Hundreds of Thousands of Millennials and Youth Come to Christ, But Ministry Far from Done." (1/14/2022) Also this interview can also be watched on "YouTube under CBN News "Innovative Ministry Helps Bring 100K+ Millennials and GenZers to Christ."

GROUNDWIRE does not call it this, but they literally have an Army of the Lord to work this process to win the GenZers and Millennials. Their approach is different, but they have already won over 100K+ of young people to the Lord through their approach. A true God given idea to bringing in the End Time Harvest.

If you have someone, or a group of young people in your church who are techy, you could add them also as a vital part of your Army of the Lord. Once they are plugged in using their gifts and talents, you could easily include them when going out into the combat zone to video and take pictures with their cell phones. They would love this. They are soldiers too! They all are representatives of the Army of the Lord.

You may have someone in your ministry a little older, who has tremendous capabilities in the technical field. They may have never thought about using their expertise to reach people who are lost and without Christ. They could be a great help by being a coach and instruct youth, college, and middle age young people who already have some skill in this area. This might be a new area of interest in your ministry with the potential to draw others in. They will be extremely effective in reaching their generation in your city in this way. Millennials and GenZer's have phenomenal ideas that will reach their generation. It will benefit your ministry by including their involvement. You will find that they will be an intricate part of reaching your community and city for Christ. Use the people that God has blessed you with and watch your ministry flourish. Encourage them to go out on the streets with you when you go. Let them feel a part by wearing their camos, hat, and Army of the Lord T-Shirt. Teach them too how to reach and win an unbeliever to Christ. They would be able to be relevant in ministering to this generation. Those people would be an asset to your entire ministry.

Everyone loves to use their phones to video and take pictures to post on social media. As they go out ministering, always ask the person(s) permission to video their conversation. Let them know it will be used to encourage the people in your ministry. Ask your soldiers to take pictures. Use everyone. When everyone returns, ask them to take their best shots and send them to your media director to use the following week to share in your service. They will be encouraged if their picture is used. They are all a part of your troop. This would involve everyone.

EQUIPPING SOLDIERS WITH TOOLS

Here is an additional conversation starter the soldiers can use. On the front of your T-Shirt on the left pocket, you will have the God Invasion Logo. Start by pointing to the logo when you walk up to someone to start a conversation. "Have you ever heard of this?" If they say, "no", you do not need to say anything about the logo. Immediately let them know your purpose for talking with them by saying. "We are here today to pray with people. Is there anything you would like for us to pray with you about?" This is always a great conversation starter and rarely will people turn you down. If someone says they don't need prayer, then use the line we taught you previously. "Would you agree with me that life has been hard? It has been a rough couple of years, right? How has that affected you?" The Holy Spirit will lead you from there.

There also may be those in your troop who during your time of prayer and intercession felt God would lead them to a specific person. Some groups call this a 'treasure hunt". Example During prayer they may feel the Holy Spirit spoke to them that they would see someone who had a yellow shirt, or who would be sitting by a water fountain, etc., and God impressed them in prayer to approach that person specifically. They may even know what they should say. This is always good, because when they go out and see exactly what God had shown them in prayer, it is a huge faith builder for that person, and for the troop. God always opens the doors. Let your soldiers interact and come up with their own unique ideas and ways.

HOW TO REACH OUR CULTURE WITH THE GOSPEL?

We are living in a unique time in America's history. This is a time when people will say they are a Christian, even if they aren't. Years ago, people would go to church even if they didn't want to. That time is over. We are living in a secular society where people have little or no knowledge of scripture whatsoever. There are many people who are completely ignorant of anything pertaining to God. Today people are in pursuit of pleasure, personal gain, and the almighty dollar is their god.

II Timothy 3 warns us what to anticipate in preparation for His Second Coming and goes into great detail what we are experiencing all over the world today. People in our society today are not pursuing God, therefore it is so important that we take God to them.

Our approach is so important! We must be anointed and equipped to handle whatever comes before us. Every soldier must know the Word of God, must be anointed for the task, and move into every situation ready to use the weapons of warfare they have been taught and given. Their personal relationship with the Lord Jesus Christ is #1. They get to know Him by fellowshipping with Him in their private prayer times. #2. They must know the Word of God, "For it is living and powerful, and sharper than any two-edged sword, piercing even to the division of the soul and spirit, and of joints and marrow, and it is a discerner of the thoughts and intents of the heart." (Hebrews 4:12 NKJV). Each soldier needs discernment in every situation. The Holy Spirit in each soldier will equip them to weigh out and discern the 'thoughts and attitudes of the hearts." Be "prayed up" has often been said, but it is so true when the soldiers' boots hit the ground and they enter the enemy's turf. We are there to take back what the devil stole from us! Each soldier's goal is to win their community. Once they win the community it will flow over into your city.

Soldiers will run into all types of people, new agers, party animals, drunks and drug addicts, highly educated people, and more. How do we reach this kind of people? The answer is the same…with the message of the gospel of Jesus Christ. He is never taken off guard, He is never taken back, He is never stumped by their questions, the soldier's weapon, God's Word, has the answer for every question that could be thrown at the soldier. They have the power of the Holy Spirit to quicken their mind and spirit. They do not need to worry about what to say, as God will give them the answer when they need it. They need to know it is not their responsibility to save them, they just need to tell them. God is the one who will lead people to the point where they want to accept Jesus as their Savior. They must know HOW to do this. There is a very well laid out and convenient app they can have downloaded on their smart phones as well. We recommend this for every soldier. It is called the "LifeOnMission" App. It is FREE, and it is a powerful tool that everyone can have available to lean on right on their smart phone if they need it.

There are several easy scriptures to memorize that will help every soldier walk an individual through the steps for salvation.

1. "For ALL have sinned and fall short of the glory of God." (Romans 3:23 NKJV)
2. "If we say we have no sin, we deceive ourselves, and the truth is not in us."
   (I John 1:8 NKJV)
3. "If we confess our sins, He is faithful and just to forgive us our sins and to cleanse us from all unrighteousness."
   (I John 1:9 NKJV)
4. 'If you will confess with your mouth that Jesus is Lord, believe in your heart that God raised Him from the dead, you will be saved. "(Romans 10:9 NKJV)
5. "Draw near to God and He will draw near to you."
   (James 4:8 NKJV)
6. "Everyone who believes in Him will never be disappointed." (Romans 10:11b TPT)
7. There are many more scriptures to be used as well, but these are fundamentals that will walk a person through to helping them understand they have sin and understand that God is the only one who can forgive them of their sin.

It is very important that each soldier understands that no one should ever try to force anyone to decide whether to accept Jesus Christ as their Savior and Lord. Lead them, guide them, but never be forceful. The decision must be theirs and from their heart. Please *don't* just say, "Hey, come to my church" etc. This will immediately turn some people away if they feel you are only trying to build your church membership. *Do* let them know you would like to connect them with some friends of yours. Tell them names, a little about each one, and really encourage them to become a part. Let them know they need friends that will stand with them in their decision, and this is just the beginning to a brand-new life.

Let them know you would like to keep in touch with them. The best way is to ask them, "Hey, will you text me? I really want to keep in touch with you." That way you can have their number in your phone and will be able to keep corresponding with them. Let them know they are important, and you want to stay connected. If you feel any uncertainty about the individual and don't want them to have your private number, ask if they have a business card, you'd like to keep in touch with them. *Do not give them your number if you feel any checks or uncertainties about them.* If they give you a card, you can turn that in to your ministries leadership / staff for them to follow up.

When you are trying to connect with them personally, these are things that will encourage new people to respond to your caring approach. They can tell if you are real and genuine or not. Relationships are important! Helping connect them to the right people will help them to grow in their new relationship with God. If you want them to come to one of your Army of the Lord meetings, by all means invite them to come. Make arrangement for them to come if they don't drive, etc. Plug them in any way you can.

If they are not coming to an Army of the Lord meeting, then we suggest the first time you meet with them, to suggest a common ground meeting place, like at a local coffee shop or restaurant. Meeting them in an open and familiar location puts everyone at ease. If they don't have transportation offer to pick them up. (Never go alone. Always take someone with you. Just let them know you wanted the person you bring along to meet them too). After you have met with them and have gotten to know them a little better, THEN invite them to your church, ministry, or group. Help them feel like you really care about them as a person, that makes them feel like you really care about them as an individual.

Some people you lead to the Lord will be zealous for God right away. They will have a heart change on the spot. Their countenance will immediately change on some, and they will have a powerful experience with God. Get their story on video with their permission, and ask them if it's okay for you to show others, your friends, etc. Encourage them to be your friend and link up through your social media, etc. The more they feel connected to you, the more they will want to be a part and join you. These are the kind of stories you want to share with your leadership.

Be sure to ask your pastor or leaders permission before hand if they would be willing to share a good converts story with the whole church, ministry, or group. Be sure to ask the new convert if they would tell their story for other people to be encouraged by. Do not put a lot of pressure on the person but explain you feel many people will be inspired by their story. Keep in touch with them during the week. Don't be overbearing but stay connected. Bible studies, prayer meetings, Army of the Lord meetings, all during the week, if they are youth, get them plugged into the youth group.

Churches, ministries, and home groups must have a way to follow up from within your ministry too. It is so important that you don't drop the new babe in Christ. Befriend them. Let them know how happy you are to hear of their decision. Help them to feel wanted and valued.

This is the way to "Start A Revival in Your City!" By all means be consistent. Do not be on one week on and off the next. Develop teams that can consistently go out on the streets, to parks, to special events that your city has, to spring and summer events, be involved, but once you start, keep steadily at it. "Be generous Invest in acts of charity, Charity yields high returns." (Ecclesiasites 1:11 MSG) Whatever a man sows, that he will also reap." (Galations 6:7 NKJV) Bad and good! It is a principle of the Word. Even if you don't see anything right away, keep on sowing, because it will come back to you. If you are sporadic at it, it will break the flow. Be consistent and stay steady at it. How can you do this? Appoint people in your ministry that can be trusted with responsibility. Structure your Army of the Lord with Captains, Lieutenants, Colonels, and Generals so each one is over a troop. If each military leader has a troop and takes one weekend a month, you will have a troop going out every week without putting an overload on your people. You will be able to give the responsibility over to individuals who have earned your trust and who you know you can depend on.

By sending one troop out a week no one gets weary from being overworked. There will be some who will want to go out every week. The idea is to keep faithful and consistent at it. Keep sending troops out, multiplication will begin to happen, and communities will be won, then you will begin to see REVIVAL starting in your CITY and your church, ministry, or home group. Get ready, because what you sow, you will reap. REVIVAL IN YOUR CITY!!!

CHAPTER 13
REAPING THE HARVEST

"We must quickly carry out the tasks assigned us by the one who sent us. The night is coming and then no one can work." (John 9:4 NLT)

"Do business til I come." (Luke 19:13b NKJV). "This is all the more urgent, for you know how late it is; time is running out. Wake up, for our salvation is nearer now than when we first believed. The night is almost gone; the day of salvation will soon be here. So remove your dark deeds like dirty clothes, and put on the shining armor of right living. Because we belong to the day, we must live decent lives for all to see. Don't participate in the darkness of wild parties and drunkenness, or in sexual promiscuity and immoral living, or quarreling and jealousy. Instead, clothe yourself with the presence of the Lord Jesus Christ. And don't let yourself think about ways to indulge your evil desires." (Romans 13:11-14 NLT).

Every soldier must be on the alert and active list. NOW IS THE TIME! We have shared with you "God's Biblical Strategy" how to "Start A Revival In Your City!" Now it is completely up to you to accept the call to respond to God's heart cry. "Thousands upon thousands are waiting in the valley of decision. There the day of the LORD will soon arrive." (Joel 3:14 NLT) "He said to his disciples, "The harvest is great, but the workers are few." (Matthew 9:37 NLT) "Then I heard the Lord asking, "Whom should I send as a messenger to this people? Who will go for Us?" (Isaiah 6:8 NLT) It is so easy to go to church, sing and play an instrument on a worship team, and to be involved in general areas serving in the ministry. Yet when it comes to two things that God calls for to start a revival in our cities, prayer and laborers in outreach, in the average ministry these areas are the least attended and supported. The average attender shows little concern for their lost loved ones, friends, co-workers and souls. This is alarming. It is up to the pastor or leader to teach your people how to reach and win new converts. Most churches have 'their own method to grow their church,' but they do not have 'God's method' to launch and start a revival in their ministry, community, and city. Many pastors and leaders today enjoy catering to their own people. Some have various forms of outreach, but there is very little involvement. Why do you think that is? Because the average attender in a ministry has no clue how to begin a conversation much less lead someone to Christ. This is seriously lacking in the majority of ministries today.

We have given you scriptures, God's heart, and the blueprint that God laid out in His Word. Raise up an Army of the Lord in YOUR church, ministry, or home group. Teach and train with the tools we have given you in this book and challenge them. Keep it continually in front of your people until it resonates in their minds, hearts, and spirits. When pastors and leaders present this before your people, and they receive clarity and instruction from God's Word week after week, their fear will dissipate, and excitement will begin to grow. Leadership will be able to clearly discern that they truly have caught the vision. You will begin to see a spark ignite their hearts. People then will catch the fire by the inner working of the Holy Spirit, who has been creating in their heart a desire to become involved. Then watch your Army of the Lord begin to rally together and grow. As they are taught 'how', something happens down deep inside their heart. As their leader, you will see them become excited about going out to win the lost.

They will become fearless warriors in their corporate world and in the marketplace because their fear of approaching and witnessing to anyone will be gone.

Keep the enthusiasm in front of your people. Stir up excitement about what is transpiring, have a day where they all wear their uniforms, and bring everyone up on the platform. Pull those who just joined to the front and introduce them as the newest soldiers, let everyone affirm them by applauds. This keeps those in the Army of the Lord excited about being a part. Create flyers and circulate them, create events inviting the whole church to become involved, have special stories shared from the platform of a soul someone has reached, and have them tell everybody their story how God has transformed their life.

Have a special event for all those who participated in reaching out to the lost. If someone has shared in the marketplace or on their job, let them 'share their story'. Keep this in front of the people consistently. The fire of sharing the gospel will catch and begin to spread like a wildfire. Celebrate their victories and wins! This is very important to keep the vitality of your troop, that could develop into troops of soul winners!

Encourage your people, even other pastors and leaders in adjoining cities next to you to buy this book. Help them start a revival in their city. There is NO COMPETITION! We are all out for souls! Every city, every church, ministry, and home group can all be inspirational in participating in a mighty move of God globally. Network and join hands together to build GOD'S Kingdom, not your own! This is a group that all will want to be a part of because they are on Fire for Jesus! Soul Winners! Working together to bring in the harvest before the Lord returns.

We encourage you to appoint Captains who will be able to teach this on a regular basis, so that new people who come in can receive the proper training and keep the troops growing and consistent with one another. You want this to be an ongoing, active, and growing ministry in your church, and in your home groups. When you put God's Biblical Strategy for revival into effect you will see results, it will grow, and you will see new people added to your church, ministry, or home group. God will bless you tremendously by using this in unifying your people to work together in service for the Commander-in-Chief who is our Lord Jesus Christ. Remember, He is the rewarder of those who diligently seek Him." (Hebrews 11:6 NKJV). Keep consistent with your weekly prayer services. This cannot stop! They are essential to keep the fires of revival burning. New faces will begin to come in. You will see new growth. The key is, do not give up. Do not quit! You are going out into a society where many hate God and do not want anything to do with Him. More times than not, you will run into many people that will be hungering for what you have to offer them. Let the soldier know that they are working for the Commander-in-Chief and He will never fail you nor forsake you, nor will He let up on that person you ministered to that may have rejected the gospel. God is faithful. He continues to work on hearts even when we are not able to. He can deal with them in their sleep, in their dreams, in their home, and even in the middle of their sin. You plant the seed and trust God. He will be faithful to send someone to water the seed that was sown, but it is always God that brings the increase! "I planted, Apollos watered, but God gave the increase." (I Corinthians 3:6b NKJV) As soldiers, we trust God and obey His commands, and we know we can trust Him with the outcome.

PREPARING WITH
WORSHIP, WORD, & SPIRITUAL WARFARE

This is a vital and extremely important step as we now are preparing to go out into the combat zone. No one knows who they will meet or what they may come up against. We have presented you with various ways and have equipped you to be a vital part of the Army of the Lord. The whole purpose of the Army of the Lord is to present the gospel to those who need Jesus and to advance the Kingdom of God.

There are 6 qualifications for each soldier to be initiated into the Troop the night of the live rehearsal. They must already have been approved by their pastor or leader.

1. Must be born again.

2. Consistently pray together with the ministry's weekly prayer group, unless their job or stated legitimate excuse prohibits them to attend regularly. This must be approved by the pastor/leader.

3. Completed all teaching/training in the Manual for 'Start A Revival in Your City

4. Purchase their own and have on their spiritual armor for the rehearsal

5. Have signed and turned in their 'Oath of Commitment' to their leader

They are now ready for practical training. This is the first night everyone will come dressed in their uniform. It creates an incredible excitement with the troop. This live training will help the soldier be more at ease before they go out into the enemy's territory. Some may still be a bit nervous and uneasy, but this trial rehearsal will help calm any anxiety they may have.

SPIRITUAL PEP RALLY

The first step is to unify the spirit of the leaders and troops, is by having an in-depth Worship, Word, and Warfare time of prayer, which is very similar to what most know as a pep rally. This is a time where everyone gets fired up to go out as a troop into their community.

WORSHIP

Have a solid time of praise and worship. If you have a worship team have them come and participate. The pastor or leader may need to suggest songs that would pertain to the evening. They need to play and sing our theme song by Carmen Licciardello's "Army of the Lord". The words are exactly who we are and what we are all about. We highly recommend this.

WORD

The pastor or leader exhorts the troop expressing the importance of the victory they are about to achieve. They literally will be going into their city, to take back what the enemy has stolen.

1. Encourage them as they prepare to go out.
2. Read a passage of scripture that will edify and build them up.
3. Display excitement in what they have been training for months to do.
4. Remind them they are going into the enemy's territory, and it truly is a combat zone, but the Holy Spirit will be going with them, and God will send His angels to oversee them.
5. They are now trained, equipped, and ready for the mission.
6. The Holy Spirit will be with them every step of the way.
7. As the leader gives a pep talk to the soldiers, speak affirmatively that we are going to **win our community for Christ and continue the mission until we take our city back for Jesus!**

8. Tell them today, we "START A REVIVAL IN OUR CITY!!

WARFARE

"You are of God, little children, and have overcome them, because He who is IN you is GREATER than he who is in the world!" (I John 4:4 NKJV) Spend quality time praying as a group together. Leaders, have specific things to pray for, like the list we have provided and suggested for you to use.

1. God's protection
2. Ask God to prepare the hearts of the people to receive Jesus
3. For the right words to say
4. Favor with those they will be contacting
5. Prayers for the right words to come into their mind as they are sharing
6. For salvations
7. And for lasting relationships to come with those they win to the Lord
8. Pray for increase in your church, ministry, or home group
9. Pray for some healings to validate the reality of Jesus to unbelievers
10. For encouraging words to flow from their mouths to the hearers
11. And pray for good connections
12. Pray for increase in your ministry

You may add additional things you feel led to pray for as well.

REHEARSAL

Break into groups of two men, or two women. Have practice runs, or trial runs. Pastors or leaders, have questions that you can pitch out to the troop. Let one soldier be the one who asks and let the other be the one who responds as if they were talking to a potential convert. Let it be a time where they start to get comfortable addressing issues, coming up with scriptures, and coming across to one another as REAL, genuine, and sincere. No church lingo, no pious answers, but real, down to earth scenarios like they might run into when they are out on the enemy's territory This practice will help to get the jitters out, and it enables them to think and process how they will handle it and respond in real situations. The soldier they are interacting with, needs to ask tough questions or things they think they might run into with real live conversations. Give them about 10-15 minutes to practice this. Switch positions and repeat the above. This can go on for some time. When the pastor or leader discerns the troop is now ready for the mission, announce it is time now to go out into the combat zone and do what we have been trained to do. Now they go with no fear because they are trained, equipped, and ready for battle!

Give any last minute 'orders' to the group before you head out. Instruct the troops to meet at a specific location in your city, at a specific time. There they all come together as an army all dressed in uniform. *No one is allowed to minister with the group unless they are dressed in full uniform and have gone through the training*. This is to keep anyone from "doing their own thing." Even if someone who wants to join and says, I was already trained in my last church." Ask if it was this specific book and program, and if so, they should have or obtain the certification or a letter of approval from their last pastor. Otherwise, before they can go out with you in the future, they must go through your training. Everyone must be trained, qualified, and unified!

Chapter 13 — REAPING THE HARVEST

When everyone arrives the pastor or leader joins with everyone in prayer, then directs them at the proper time to break up and go out on the mission in two's.

1. Remind them where they are all to return and meet at a specific time.
2. Make sure you count heads before they leave and when they return.
3. You must be sure you have every single soldier accounted for.
4. Upon return, have them 'share their stories' of what took place while they were out, and let that excitement grow.
5. Close in prayer and announce before you leave "when, where, and what time" you will be meeting again the following week. Give detailed orders to the whole troop while they still are all together. It is so important NOT to lose momentum from the event. Keep the flow moving forward!
6. Pastor and leader, let them know when you will be gathering their information, and specifically when you will be gathering the names of those who accepted the Lord as their Savior.
7. Follow up is a mandate.
8. You may coordinate this in whatever is the best way for your ministry to care for these new converts.
9. Whatever you do, DON'T DROP THEM!
10. When you all meet again specifically pray over those names.
11. Assign names to soldiers to specifically pray for throughout the week. They need to be followed up with **that same week!**
12. Close in prayer and ask everyone to join with you asking that the Spirit of the Lord continue to speak to

hearts and their spirit, ask the Holy Spirit to draw others to the saving knowledge of the Lord Jesus Christ.

Remember, after they have gone out, in your next Sunday service have a couple of people 'share their story' and experience. Have the whole church or ministry pray together and give thanks for what the Lord has done!

Again, keeping this in front of your people will encourage them to continue to see, hear, and create a desire to be a part of the 'Big Thing' that God is doing in your ministry.

CHAPTER 14

GOD INVASION - RELEASING REVIVAL

"Blow the trumpet in Zion and sound an alarm in My holy mountain! Let all the inhabitants of the land tremble; For the day of the Lord is coming, for it is at hand." (Joel 2:1 NKJV)

America and the whole world are reeling from the strikes of the enemy. He is in an all-out attack globally. He knows that the coming of the Lord is nearby. "A day of darkness and gloominess, a day of clouds and thick darkness, like the morning clouds spread over the mountains. A people come, great and strong, the like of whom has never been; Nor will there ever be any such after them, even for many successive generations. A fire devours before them, and behind them a flame burns; The land is like the Garden of Eden before them, and behind them a desolate wilderness; Surely nothing shall escape them. Their appearance is like the appearance of horses; and like swift steeds, so they run. With a noise like chariots over mountaintops they leap, like the noise of flaming fire that devours the stubble, like a strong people set in battle array. Before them the people writhe in pain; All faces are drained of color. They run like mighty men, they climb the wall like men of war; everyone marches in formation, and they do not break ranks. They do not push one another; Everyone marches in his own column. Though they lunge between the weapons, they are not cut down. They run to and fro in the CITY, they run on the wall; they climb into the houses, they enter at the windows like a thief. The earth quakes before them, the heavens tremble; the sun and moon grow dark, and the stars diminish their brightness. The LORD GIVES VOICE BEFORE <u>HIS ARMY,</u> FOR HIS CAMP IS VERY GREAT; For STRONG is the ONE who executes His word. For the day of the Lord is great and very terrible who can endure it?" (Joel 2:2-11 NKJV)

This is a declaration from the Word of God. He has promised that "No weapon formed against you shall prosper." (Isaiah 54:17a NKJV). The Army of the Lord goes out strong, and they are powerful, and their swords are sharper than any two-edged sword.

A CALL TO REPENTANCE

"Now, therefore," says the Lord, Turn to Me with all your heart, With fasting, with weeping and with mourning. So, rend your heart, and not your garments; Return to the Lord your God, For He is gracious and merciful, Slow to anger, and of great kindness; And He relents from doing harm. Who knows if He will turn and relent, and leave a blessing behind Him – A grain offering and a drink offering for the Lord your God? BLOW THE TRUMPET IN ZION." (Joel 2:12-15a NKJV).

This Word is clear. When the Army of the Lord moves forward into the combat zone, they will be releasing a mighty move of God that will burst forth into a revival. God goes ahead of His mighty soldiers and invades the land, and revival is birthed!

THE LAND REFRESHED

"Then the Lord will be zealous for His land, and pity His people. The Lord will answer and say to His people, "Behold I will send you grain and new wine and oil, and you will be satisfied by them; I will no longer make you a reproach among the nations. But I will remove far from you the northern army, and will drive him away into a barren and desolate land, with his face toward the eastern sea and his back toward the western sea..." (Joel 2:18-20 NKJV)

"Fear not, O land; be glad and rejoice, for the Lord has done marvelous things! Do not be afraid" (Joel 2:21-22a NKJV) "Be glad then, you children of Zion, and rejoice in the Lord your God; for He has given you the former rain faithfully, and He will cause the rain to come down for you - the former rain, and the latter rain in the first month. The threshing floors shall be full of wheat, and the vats shall overflow with new wine and oil. So, I will restore to you the years that the swarming locust has eaten..." (Joel 2:21a-23b NKJV)

We are to rejoice in the Lord! "...My great ARMY which I sent AMONG YOU. You shall eat in plenty and be satisfied, and praise the name of the Lord your God, who has dealt wondrously with you And My people shall never be put to shame. Then you shall know that I AM in the midst of Israel; I AM the Lord your God, and there is none other. My people shall never be put to shame." (Joel 2:23b, -25d-27 NKJV)

GOD'S SPIRIT POURED OUT

'And IT SHALL COME TO PASS AFTERWARD, THAT I WILL <u>POUR OUT MY SPIRIT ON ALL FLESH;</u> your sons and your daughter shall prophesy, your old men shall dream dreams, Your young men shall see visions. And also on My menservants and on My maidservants I WILL POUR OUT MY SPIRIT IN THOSE DAYS." (Joel 2:28-29 NKJV) For those who may say, "that is in the Old Testament, that's not for today." Here in the New Testament a verse saying very close to the same thing. "And it shall come to pass in the last days, says God, That I WILL POUR

Chapter 14 — GOD INVASION - RELEASING REVIVAL

OUT OF MY SPIRIT ON ALL FLESH; Your sons and your daughters shall prophesy, your young men shall see visions, Your old men shall dream dreams, and on My menservants and maidservants I will pour out My Spirit in those days; and they shall prophesy." (Acts 2:17 NKJV)

These are all promises from God. We have the assurance from God Himself, that if we apply His Biblical Strategy for revival, we will see it! We will be a part of it! You will "START A REVIVAL IN YOUR CITY!"

Our nations' conscience is hardened just as it was in the day of Elijah. Elijah had a burden for his country because Ahab was turning the whole country to Baal. Are we not seeing this same thing in America today? Indifference rules, lawlessness rules, but God says in His Word that what He has planned is, "not by might, nor by power, but BY MY SPIRIT SAYS THE LORD of hosts." (Zechariah 4:6 NKJV). When we go out as an ARMY OF THE LORD we will take back what the enemy has stolen from us. We will win back communities, cities, and nations! We cannot do this on our own, it will take an Army of the Lord forming all over the world to win the lost and reclaim the territory that belongs to GOD!!!

Today in America and around the world, people's opinions vacillate and they are strongly opposing the truths established in God's Word. For this reason, desperate spiritual measures must be taken because these types of attitudes prevail everywhere. God will be using our soldiers of the Lord to give *visual evidence* to unbelievers, and even to believers who doubt, to awaken those who claim to be woke. God will give us power to provide evidence that our God is undeniable, and our God's power is real.

Proof has been given in creation alone. But God will provide in the days ahead, fresh visual evidence as proof to those who refuse to believe He exists, as well as to convict those who are passive and wavering. We must understand that God never intended for visual demonstrations of spiritual power to produce permanent change. God uses them to prick the conscience that temporarily activates the submissive will, and then the Holy Spirits ability to offer conviction, which leads to repentance and conversion. This is God's plan for dealing with and confronting those whose hearts are hardened.

As the Army of the Lord goes forth in God's power and in His might, they are going to not just see, but they are going to BE a part of God's hand extended to a world who have hardened their hearts to things of God. As each soldier allows the Holy Spirit to flow through them as a yielded vessel, God will do mighty things through them. It is of utmost importance that no one ever take the glory that belongs to God. He may have used you, but you have no ability on your own to perform the things that He has in mind to reach our hardened world. Watch your heart, soldier. Never, ever take glory for anything that God will do through you because you are a yielded vessel, equipped and trained to be a small part of a bigger army that will spread across the land. All praise and all honor MUST GO to Him who saw you fit to be used for His Kingdoms purpose.

God will be using the Army of the Lord to do mighty and great exploits to validate who He is, and to give validation to those who do not believe that He is alive and well.

A God Invasion is getting ready to happen in YOUR CITY! Be humbled by the fact that God has chosen you to be a part of the End Time Revival that He is ushering in. God is going to use the leaders and people in the Army of the Lord to release revival and it is going to spread from communities, to cities, and to nations. Once this fire begins to spread there will be no stopping it. It will burn until Jesus splits the sky and takes us all home to be with

Him. Attention Soldiers, "And let us not grow weary while doing good, for in due season we shall reap if we do not lose heart. Therefore, as we have opportunity, let us do good to all, especially to those who are of the household of faith." (Galations 6:9 NKJV)

God will RELEASE REVIVAL in your community and city as you follow God's Biblical Strategy and blueprint for a powerful, authentic, move of God. The TIME IS NOW!!! Together we can make a difference for such a time as this!

CHAPTER 15

"A CHRISTIAN REVIVAL REVOLUTION"

"Then I will sprinkle clean water on you, and you shall be clean; I will cleanse you from all your filthiness and from all your idols. I will give you a new heart and put a new spirit within you; I will take the heart of stone out of your flesh and give you a heart of flesh." (Ezekiel 36:25-26 NKJV)

Revival will happen when God's people are prepared. It happens when we have spent time in prayer, fasting, searching and cleansing our spirit while waiting on God, which forms a tender heart and a humble spirit. We cannot orchestrate widespread, far-reaching revival alone. We do our part that He has given us in His Word through His Biblical Strategy for revival, then He does His part. He has clearly told us to raise up an Army of the Lord! As we obey all of His commands that He has given us, then He brings the results. Revival!

Born-again believers who have been involved in the church world know the Scripture found in (II Chronicles 7:14 NKJV). We have it all down well except one part! "If MY PEOPLE (of course that's us), who are called by MY NAME (that is every born again believer), will humble themselves, and pray and seek My face, (we have gotten this part down pretty well) and TURN FROM THEIR

WICKED WAYS," (This is the part where we are truly lacking), because He goes on to say, "THEN I will hear from heaven, and will forgive <u>their</u> sin and HEAL <u>THEIR</u> LAND." The problem is that many in the church world today, have no clue what 'sin' is because they have not heard much preaching on this topic. Maybe a few things, but for the most 'sin' is not addressed. Does the Bible not say that "MY PEOPLE are destroyed for the lack of knowledge?" (Hosea 4:6 NKJV) It is very possible that the coming worldwide revival will start through the Army of the Lord's global army in churches, para-church ministries, marketplace, and expand out into nations?

What are some "Christian sins" that we need to confess? I truly believe if some of these things were preached about in love and not through accusation, God could move and begin a revival in the church. Many true believers do not know where to begin when it comes to searching their hearts. They do not sin willfully, so they honestly do not know of any sin that they are consciously aware of.

Reading scriptures helps to identify sin in our heart that we need to repent of. Listed below are a just 'few' sins that pastors and leaders could, and or should, preach about to help believers self-examine their own heart. When we repent from our heart this can begin to turn the tide of revival!

CREATE IN ME A CLEAN HEART

We should pray as Psalmist David prayed, "Create in me a clean heart, O God. Renew a loyal spirit within me." (Psalm 51:10 NLT) Below are a few things to ponder and consider as we pray and search our hearts before God.

<u>PRAYERLESSNESS</u>

Is sin against the Lord

"Moreover, as for me, far be it from me that I should sin against the Lord in ceasing to pray for you; but I will teach you the good and the right way." (I Samuel 12:23 NKJV)

PRIDE

God hates pride

"The Lord detests the proud; they will surely be punished." (Proverbs 16:5 NLT)

LUST FOR SEX

"Your ancestors have been taught, 'Never commit adultery.' However, I say to you if you <u>look</u> with lust in your eyes at a woman who is not your wife, you've already committed adultery in your heart." (Matthew 5:27-29 TPT)

LUST FOR MONEY

"Loving money is a root of all evils. Some people run after it so much that they have given up their faith. Craving more money pushes them away from the faith into error, compounding misery in their lives." (I Timothy 6:10-20 TPT)

COVETOUSNESS

Means having an insatiable appetite or desire for worldly gain, also trying to find purpose in things instead of God.

"Don't love the world's ways. Don't love the world's goods. Love of the world squeezes out love for the Father. Practically everything that goes on in the world – wanting your own way, wanting everything for yourself, wanting to appear important - has nothing to do with the Father. It just isolates you from Him, the world and all its wanting, wanting, wanting is on the way out – but whoever does what God wants is set for eternity." (I John 2:15-17 MSG)

BACKBITER

A person who says ugly things about a person behind their back

"And never let ugly or hateful words come from your mouth, but instead let your words become beautiful gifts that encourage others; do this by speaking words of grace to help them." (Ephesians 4:29 TPT)

DISUNITY, JEALOSY, ANGRY OUTBURSTS, SELFISH AMBITION, SLANDER, GOSSIP, ARROGANCE, AND TURMOIL

"Now I'm afraid that when I come to you I may find you different than I desire you to be, and you may find me different than you would like me to be. I don't want to find you in disunity, with jealousy and angry outbursts, with selfish ambition, slander, gossip, arrogance, and turmoil. I'm actually afraid that on my next visit my God will humble me in front of you as I shed tears over those who keep sinning without repenting of their impurity, sexual immorality, and perversion." (II Corinthians 12:20-21 TPT)

"You have not repented of your impurity, sexual immorality, and eagerness for lustful pleasure." (II Corinthians 12:21b NLT)

ADULTERY

Sex between a married person and someone other than their spouse

"You must not commit adultery." (Exodus 20:14 NLT)

"Whoever commits adultery with a woman lacks understanding. He who does so destroys his own soul." (Proverbs 6:32 NKJV)

FORNICATION – WORKS OF THE FLESH

Fornication is sexual activity between two people who are not married to each other.

"Now the works of the flesh are evident, which are adultery, fornication, uncleanness, lewdness, idolatry, sorcery, hatred, contentions, jealousies, outburst of wrath, selfish ambitions, dissensions, heresies, envy murders, drunkenness, revelries, and the like of which I tell you beforehand, just as I also told you in time past, that those who practice such thigs will not inherit the kingdom of God." (Galations 5:19-21 NKJV)

(*Suggestion: Pastors and leaders you can take each word, give definition of each, and preach on each one in a series. Powerful!)

BITTERNESS

A person who is angry, cannot put bad things that happened to them in the past behind them. Remembers details of past hurt and holds unforgiveness. Often wants to retaliate against the person that hurt them.

"Watch out that no poisonous root of bitterness grows up to trouble you, corrupting many." (Hebrews 12:15b NLT)

COMPLAINING

"Do everything without complaining and arguing, so that no one can criticize you. Live clean, innocent lives as children of God, shining like bright lights in a world full of crooked and perverse people. Hold firmly to the word of life; then, on the day of Christ's return, I will be proud that I did not run the race in vain and that my work was not useless." (Philippians 2:14-16 NLT)

DECEITFULNESS & A LYING TONGUE

Deceitful Someone who hides the truth, especially to gain an advantage "So, get rid of all evil behavior. Be done with all deceit, hypocrisy, jealousy, and all unkind speech." (I Peter 2:1 NLT)

"There are six things that the Lord hates – no, seven things He detests; 'haughty eyes, a lying tongue, hands that kill the innocent, a heart that plots evil, feet that race to do wrong, a false witness who pours out lies; a person who sows discord in a family." (Proverbs 6:16-19 NLT)

OVERINDULGENCE

"When you discover something sweet, don't overindulge and eat more than you need, for excess in anything can make you sick of even a good thing" (Proverbs 25:16 TPT)

ENVY

"Do not let you heart envy sinners but be zealous for the fear of the Lord all the day." (Proverbs 23:17 NKJV)

HATRED

"He who hates, disguises it with his lips, and lays up deceit withing himself." (Proverbs 26:24 NKJV)

KNOWING TO DO GOOD BUT DOES NOT DO IT

When a person knows something is wrong, but they go ahead and do it anyway.

"Therefore, to him who knows to do good and does not do it, to him it is sin." (James 4:17 NKJV)

LYING

"Don't steal. Don't lie. Don't deceive anyone." (Leviticus 19:11 MSG)

"Lying lips are an abomination to the Lord, but those who deal truthfully are His delight." (Proverbs 12:22 NKJV)

CHEATING

"God hates cheating in the marketplace; he loves it when business is aboveboard." (Proverbs 11:1 MSG)

SLANDER AGAINST A BROTHER OR SISTER

Slander is a false spoken statement said to purposefully damage a person's reputation.

"So clean house! Make a clean sweep of malice and pretense, envy and hurtful talk." (I Peter 2:1-2a MSG)

SPEAKING EVIL AGAINST GOD'S MESSENGER

"Don't bad-mouth your leaders, not even under your breath, and don't abuse your betters, even in the privacy of your home. Loose talk has a way of getting picked up and spread around. Little birds drop the crumbs of your gossip far and wide." (Ecclesiastes 10:20 MSG)

UNBELIEF

"…because they did not believe the love of the truth, that they might be saved. And for this reason, God will send them strong delusion, that they should believe the lie that they all may be condemned who did not believe the truth but had pleasure in unrighteousness."
(II Thessalonians 2:9b –12 NKJV)

These are just starters in God's Word that we can all start with. There are so many more scriptures that reveal sin that can be hidden in our hearts. They have to be preached from a loving heart with an anointing that comes only through one's personal prayer life. There can be no judgment mixed in, only the pure Word of God. Until the people of God truly repent, according to (II Chronicles 7:14) and *"turn from their wicked ways,"* we will not see our ***land healed***. This is very important as we go out on the streets to win those who are lost. The two together, (1) examining our own hearts and truly repenting, and (2) going out with the Army of the Lord reaching the unsaved, will lead us all into revival, both personally and corporately.

Chapter 15   "A CHRISTIAN REVIVAL REVOLUTION"

Revival comes when the Word of God is preached with a supernatural anointing. The Holy Spirit sends deep inner conviction to the listeners. True repentance is when there is a sincere, genuine remorse for the sin or sins that one has committed, along with a clear understanding that it has tremendously grieved the heart of God. When people clearly understand this, they respond sincerely from their heart, and a change of behavior follows. People who know them can observe and witness a transformation. This is powerful evidence to unbelievers of the reality and the power of a living God.

When revival comes to a church, ministry, or home group, God releases a wave of His Spirit through the people. A genuine spirit of God's power surges through those present, and their focus moves completely to God, and God alone. They recognize and respond to the promptings of the Holy Spirit and a movement begins.

We do not have to question whether or not God wants us to reach our city. He tells us when the Spirit of the Lord God is upon us, we go forth in power and under His guidance and anointing. "The Spirit of the Lord God is upon Me, because the Lord has anointed Me to preach good tidings to the poor; He has sent Me to heal the brokenhearted, to proclaim liberty to the captives, and the opening of the prison to those who are bound; to proclaim the acceptable year of the Lord, And the day of vengeance of our God; To comfort all who mourn, to console those who mourn in Zion, To give them beauty for ashes, the oil of joy for mourning, the garment of praise for the spirit of heaviness; that they may be called trees of righteousness, The planting of the Lord, that HE MAY BE GLORIFIED." (Isaiah 61:1-3 NKJV)

He tells us in the same passage, "The Spirit of God, the Master, is on me because God anointed me. He sent me to preach good news to the poor, heal the heartbroken, announce freedom to all captives, pardon all prisoners. God sent me to announce the year of His grace–a celebration of God's destruction of our enemies–and to comfort all who mourn, To care for the needs of all who mourn in Zion, give them bouquets of roses instead of ashes, Messages of joy instead of news of doom, a praising heart instead of languid spirit. Rename them "Oaks of Righteousness" planted by God to display His glory." (Isaiah 61:1-9 MSG). "And seek the peace of the CITY where I have caused you to be carried away captive, and pray to the Lord for it; for in its peace you will have peace. (Jeremiah 29:6b -7 NKJV). Another translation in that same verse says, "They will rebuild the ancient ruins, repairing cities destroyed long ago. They will revive them, though they have been deserted for many generations. (Isaiah 61:4 NLT)

The Spirit of the Lord is upon this Army of the Lord who are end time revivalists, and they will be able to effectively minister to those who are grieving and mourning. They will interact and exchange with people by the power of God. They will see God exchange the sorrowful heart for a heart of rejoicing.

Soldiers will have a supernatural anointing by God to go bring in the lost. "For God did not send His Son into the world to condemn the world, but that the world through Him might be saved." (John 3:17 NKJV)

In essence the troops are preparing the way of the Lord. There is a great divide between sinners and God. As the Army of the Lord, we all work together to bridge this gap and build a road to revival. This prepares the way for man and God to connect. Just as John the Baptist preached, he built a road and bridge in his message that prepared people for Jesus. Of course, his message was one of repentance. When anyone repents immediately a road is built out of the rubble of their sin immediately to God. This is what paves the way for a revival.

The Army of the Lord can be sure that the Lord will go before them, and "The eternal God is your refuge, and underneath are the everlasting arms He will thrust out the enemy from before you and will say, "Destroy!" (Deuteronomy 33:27 NKJV). He is "The shield of your help and the sword of your majesty! Your enemies shall submit to you, and you shall tread down their high places." (Deuteronomy 33:29 NKJV)

Soldiers, have every right to claim your city for Jesus. God keeps His covenant for thousands of generations. You will also have favor with authorities in your land. "And He will deliver their kings into your hand, and you will destroy their name from under heaven; no one shall be able to stand against you until you have destroyed them." (Deuteronomy 7:24 NKJV) God is giving you authority over your city. Handle it with genuine sincerity and with the love of God that resides in your heart. Jesus too felt the importance of preaching in cities. "Now it came to pass, when Jesus finished commanding His twelve disciples, that He departed from there to teach and to preach in their cities." (Matthew 11:1 NKJV)

REVIVAL

A true revival is birthed with much prayer and this is the foundation on which it is built. Revival does not come easy. We all press in together with pastors, leaders, and with your core troop of soldiers. You move forward and together, pursue God consistently. You will find yourself praying often and sacrificially. You are drawn to obey God at all costs. As you pray privately and with your core troop of soldiers, this is where the atmosphere lends itself to the Spirit of God. When people pray and begin to search their own heart, often tears begin to fall as they recognize the presence of God surrounding them in a tangible way. When this happens one begins to repent humbly and genuinely to God. This is very important as it keeps all of our hearts softened to the voice of God, and to hearing clearly His voice.

Revival is not easy! Revival takes persistence individually to touch God, and a determination to press in with a longing for Him to breathe His presence fresh on you every day. When God's Spirit truly targets and impacts one's heart then dedication follows. During this process you will find yourself emptying out everything that has caused you to waver in things of God. There is a release to Him of things that have caused you to drift away or stumble in your walk with God. There is a strong pull and desire to let go of those things that you once thought were important and took God's place in your life. It is coming to a place where you willfully allow God to have His complete way in your life.

In the process God will tear down walls that we thought would protect us, but didn't. He will leave our soul laying bare before a pure and Holy God. It is then and only then, that He can pour Himself into an empty vessel so that we can become everything He wants us to be.

Pastors, leaders, and soldiers, are we eagerly anticipating a fresh and authentic move of God? Throughout the years I have been around people who long to see *a repeat* of what transpired in the revivals of centuries long ago, The Great Awakenings, and more recently The Brownsville Revival. They truly were God ordained and were true moves of God. They were very powerful and life changing. A wonderful time that many of us had the privilege of experiencing and will never forget. We feel privileged to have been a part of such a tremendous and life impacting experience. But it is in the past now.

Every previous revival from centuries ago with Jonathan Edwards, John Wesley, George Whitfield, Charles Finney, the Welsh Revival, the Asuza Street Revival with William J. Seymour, and so many, many others all started with intense prayer times and meetings. The most resent and well-known Pensacola Outpouring or Brownsville Revival with Evangelist Steve Hill was used by God to bring a mighty move of God where the estimated 2.5 million - 4.5 million who attended. Once again, it all began with prayer. Pastor John Kilpatrick the pastor of Brownsville Assembly of God in Pensacola, Florida prayed for 2 years asking God to bring revival and God answered the cry of his heart. So, people have patterned their lives and ministries after what they have read, and or witnessed. They truly are good examples for all of us, but if this was the only thing that will bring revival, we should be seeing the evidence of that by now. Thousands and even millions have been praying and still are praying. As we have said before, **prayer is the key to revival**. Yes! It is! But the 'new thing' that God is desiring is to bring unity between believers, who will join hands together to win the world for the Kingdom of God. Their 'doctrines' may be different than yours, but can we not agree on one point, that Jesus died to save all sinners to **build the Kingdom of God**? Can we lay down our differences and work together to see souls come into the Kingdom? Born again believers, pastors, leaders, churches, ministries, home groups, we all need to drop our differences and join hands to win the world. Let's build the Kingdom of God together. I repeat, there is no competition in this coming move of God! EVERY CITY that has people praying and believing, seeking the heart of God, and wants to see their communities and cities won to the Lord, can have a full churches and assemblies. Isn't that what every leader wants? With the internet we all can expand our tent pegs and win our world!!! There is NO COMPETITION!

At times throughout decades there has been a competitive spirit in the hearts of some leaders concerning their ministry. They do not want to 'cross pollinate' with other ministries. They want to remain isolated and not join hands with others who have a heart for winning the lost. There is no way in the world that God is going to honor that. There is only one God, one Savior, and one Heaven. EVERY CITY can experience a revival and genuine move of God! The verse in Isaiah clearly says two important things. One, "Behold, I am doing a NEW THING, NOW it shall spring forth; shall you no know it?" Two, "We are to forget the past", (not what He did, but HOW He did it,) because He is "doing a NEW THING and NOW it shall spring forth." (Isaiah 43:18-19 NKJV) For clarity once again, if you study that verse that says 'forget the past" remember we shared what the actual Hebrew words mean, don't forget those wonderful times and what God did, but forget HOW He did it. When we keep wanting it to happen like it did back then, we are limiting God. God is specifically telling us that He is wanting to do a "NEW THING."

This concept of setting cities on fire for God all over the USA and into other nations is a NEW THING. It has the capacity to reach the world. Brownsville was another wonderful and truly authentic move of God. Innumerable lives were touched and changed, and many who went still feel the impact of those days. But God is not going to do it like He did back then. People came from other nations and from all over the United States and went back and impacted their ministries. Don't you see, God's vision is bigger now! Many people have prepared their hearts for years and are still praying for revival. This NEW revival is going to involve the body of Christ. He is desiring for all of us to impact people in the marketplace, workplace, schools, universities, and everywhere!

We see the need all around us every day. Greater then any of us have ever imagined especially in the past few of years. Satan is pulling out all stops to do whatever necessary to take souls to hell for eternity. Satanism, witchcraft, illuminati. ouija boards, tarot cards, fortune tellers are drawing people by the pull of the demonic world in which they tamper. This is not something we can shrug off any longer. God wants to raise up Armies of the Lord all over the world. "Heaven suffers violence and the violent take it by force." (Matthew 11:12b NKJV) What is meant by this verse? John the Baptist had crowds that literally flocked to him in the desert when he was preaching there. He was a fearless preacher who was a simple man of God whose life was surrounded by worldly people. He was a messenger that prepared the way of the Lord. From the very beginning of John's ministry the Scribes and Pharisees had vigorously opposed his message. King Herod did all he could to fight and oppose his preaching of the Word. Where it talks about "the violent take it by force" the King and the Scribes and Pharisees did their very best to take the kingdom down in order to destroy it. Men would hammer at it from the outside, trying to get in. They wanted to bust the doors down to get in. So, the interpretation is that John's preaching touched off violent reactions with widespread, deep, and lasting effects. In this day and age, we are living in, we see people all around us everywhere who are trying to take God out of everything, along with trying to remove the Word of God, churches, ministries, etc. We must raise up and Army of the Lord to combat the enemy and his territory. We too, with God on our side, can take it back by force!

We have a reason to fight today. Sin like in Sodom and Gomorrah in America and worldwide is great, even worse! But no sin is greater than the power of the living God. Soldiers, you must be convinced of this in your hearts, minds, and spirit. The power in you is greater than the power in them. Do not think that Satan does not have power because you are gravely mistaken. BUT...there is far more POWER in the Blood of Jesus! Demons have to submit to the name of Jesus. They have to cease their attack when the power of Jesus is released upon them. So soldier and troops you do not have to be afraid. God is greater! His POWER is greater!

As a soldier, if you come into contact with a person who is demonically controlled, use the name of Jesus, apply the blood of Jesus, and the power of His Word, and the enemy will flee. They will be freed from the grip the enemy had on their life! "For the message of the cross is foolishness to those who are perishing, but to us who are being saved it is the power of God." (I Corinthians 1:18 NKJV).

CHAPTER 16

WALKING IN THE SUPERNATURAL POWER OF GOD

"Whoever believes the good news and is baptized will be saved, and whoever does not believe the good news will be condemned. And these miracle signs will accompany those who believe They will drive our demons in the power of my name. They will speak in tongues. They will be supernaturally protected from snakes and from drinking anything poisonous. And they will lay hands on the sick and heal them." (Mark 16:16-18 TPT)

As soldiers of the cross you will experience signs, wonders, and miracles as you go about God's business. It is important to understand their usage because God Himself validated His message many times using signs, wonders, and with various kinds of miracles. Also, pursue the value of having the gift of the Holy Spirit. Let us break them down to understand as follows:

SIGNS

Signs were those miracles that were performed by the Lord and by the apostles. The signs were those miracles that were distinct in physical form that indicated spiritual truths as referenced in (John 6:1-14 NKJV) with the feeding of the five thousand. He gave an illustration concerning the Bread of Life as found in (John 6:25-59 NKJV). So, the Lord would use 'signs' as a means to illustrate His Word giving a clear spiritual implication.

WONDERS

'Wonders' were miracles that were used to arouse amazement in those who were there spectating. An example would be of the raising of Lazarus from the dead. This definitely aroused the curiosity of all those who were present to witness this event. People undoubtedly witnessed a true miracle that day, what was and is impossible with man, ALL things are possible with God. They stood in amazement as they watched the dead man come to life and hop out into the open, wrapped in grave clothes. When they unraveled the garment, Lazarus was very much alive. (John 11:1- 44 NKJV)

MIRACLES

Miracles are any type of displays of supernatural power that clashed with the laws of nature. This would be anything that was impossible in the natural, was made possible by God's supernatural power only! The purpose of all the miracles performed in the Bible was to prove the truth of the gospel, not to pump any man's ego, but to clearly present Jesus as being the One that defied all laws of nature. One example is found in (Matthew 14:22-36 NKJV) Jesus walked across the Sea of Galilee. Just one of many examples.

GIFTS OF THE HOLY SPIRIT

Gifts of the Holy Spirit are special moments given to men and women to speak and act in a way that is completely beyond their natural abilities.

As soldiers go out to invade the powers of darkness, the Holy Spirit is going to be enabling numerous believers with miraculous powers, to validate to unbelievers that God is real. He exists today and will let them know that they can believe in God because He is alive and real. Miraculous powers are given out by the Holy Spirit as He chooses.

"And these signs will follow those who believe in My name they will cast out demons; they will speak with new tongues; they will take up serpents; and if they drink anything deadly, it will by no means hurt them; they will lay hands on the sick, and they will recover."(Mark 16:17-18 NKJV) "Then God blessed them, and God said to them, "Be fruitful and multiply; fill the earth and subdue it; have dominion over the fish of the sea, over the birds of the air, and over every living thing that moves on the earth." (Genesis 1:28 NKJV).

HEALINGS

As stated in earlier chapters we are told in His Word that we are going to do greater works then Jesus did. Perhaps that is due to the fact that there are unique and completely different challenges in our day as was in Jesus'. "Most assuredly, I say to you, he who believes in Me, the works that I do he will do also; and greater works than these he will do, because I go to My Father. And whatever you ask in My name, that I will do, that the Father may be glorified in the Son. If you ask anything in My name. I will do it." (John 14:12 NKJV). The key is to believe in Him and have no doubt that He is able.

All genuine healing comes from God. If you have ever been sick and have experienced the healing power of God, you can truly say you believe and know that He is able. (Psalm 103 NKJV) tells us of all the benefits we receive as believers. We learn that the Lord is able to heal all kinds of diseases. There is nothing with

Jesus that is an incurable disease. He says, "you will lay hands on the sick and they will recover." (Mark 16:18d NKJV). Expect to be used of God in this way and understand that God will use it to validate Him to the unbeliever, they will have no doubt that He is real. We see this in (Acts 2:22 NKJV) "Men of Israel, hear these words Jesus of Nazareth, a Man attested (means He provided evidence, why? to declare something exists, a testimony, to verify) by God to you by miracles, wonders, and signs which God did through Him in your midst, as you yourselves also know – Him..." Remember, real is what people today want to see, especially the Millennials and GenXers. God will go before you. Listen to His voice and when He tells you specifically to pray, be obedient and watch God work. This is another weapon and tool the Lord gives to His soldiers to equip them *to validate* God's presence and existence. He can heal on the spot with a miracle, or over a period of time, however He chooses. No limit can be placed on His healing.

Another group to be on the lookout for are the God defiers. They are truly out there today. This gives one the greatest opportunities for God to demonstrate His power. We find tremendous examples of this in the story concerning David and the giant Goliath.

We find when David fought Goliath and won, that he addressed this giant when Goliath mocked David for his size and his unusual weapon. What was David's response? "Then David said to the Philistine, 'You come to me with a sword and spear, and battle-ax. I come to you in the name of God-of-the-Angel-Armies, the God of Israel's troops, whom you curse and mock." (I Samuel 17:45-47 MSG) David was distraught that Goliath was defying the Lord his God, and God observed that, and gave David the ability and favor to take the giant down and win the battle.

Also, in I Kings 18 Elijah saw where indifference ruled. The people were vacillating between two opinions and as a result the country of Israel's conscience had hardened. Ahab was leading this country down the wrong path and they were turning to Baal, who of course represented Satan. Again, like Goliath mocked David, Ahab mocked Elijah and called him a 'trouble maker." Deception will cause unbelievers to believe a lie from the enemy.

Elijah was not detoured in the least by Ahab's verbal attacks. He was close to God, and he took on the challenge of Ahab and his false prophets. They had torn down the altars, and Elijah went in with the purpose of rebuilding God's altar.

They were also in a drought. Elijah knew how big his God was, and he also knew that God was behind his purpose. He challenged Ahab and all the false prophets. He let Ahab and all the false prophets cry out to their gods to prove their gods did not hear them. He clearly recognized the broken down boundaries of the national conscience when no one else around him would take the responsibility. He went boldly and set the stage. He quietly rebuilt the broken down altar. He used twelve stones which signified the twelve tribes. Baal's prophets cried out to their god for hours. Nothing. Elijah even made fun of them for believing in a god that had no power. So, as he built the altar, he dug a trench around it and insulted them by bringing in twelve barrels of water in the middle of their 3-year drought and had them pour it over the bull they had placed and cut up on the altar. The water ran down into the trenches. It saturated the animal as well. As Elijah prayed, he acknowledged the sins of the twelve tribes. Pouring the water represented and symbolized repentance. After Baals prophets had cried out for hours and even cut themselves until blood flowed, nothing was happening.

Elijah stepped forward after making it as hard as possible from their perspective for his God to do anything. As Elijah stepped forward and said a simple prayer, God heard, and it brought down a heavenly display that those people had never seen before in their lives. The Fire Fell! It licked up every drop of water, burnt the wood, even burned up the stones on the altar as well as the sacrifice. What was the result? The unbelievers cried out, "We want your God!!!" They doubted no longer and left Ahab's and their god for Elijah's God. When God has someone He knows He can trust, He will give a plan. If we obey Him and Set It Up, we can trust God to Show Up! (I Kings 18 NKJV)

I ask this question with all sincerity in my heart. Church people, what has happened to us? And "when" did it happen to us? Where we would rather coddle a sinning saint and wink at their sin, rather than embrace and weep over a sinner? Where did things take a turn when we, "the Church" started to glamorize sin, accept sinful conduct, and feel we are sanctified, and justify our sinful behaviors, and give the concept that it is ok?

Are we guilty of this very thing of winking at sin and telling people they are ok; they are under grace? Yes, we are under grace but that does not give us the right to crucify Christ again. No wonder God Word says, "If MY PEOPLE who are called by MY NAME will humble themselves, and pray and Seek My face, and ***TURN FROM THEIR WICKED WAYS, THEN*** I will hear from heaven, and forgive their sin and ***HEAL their land***." (II Chronicles 7:14 NKJV). Have you ever noticed that so many times when we quote this verse, we leave out one of the most important essentials of God's criteria? ***"TURN FROM THEIR WICKED WAYS"*** ...***THEN*** I will hear from heaven, will forgive their sin and ***heal their land***." I know I have emphasized this all throughout this book, but it is so important that we get this!

ATTENTION! We are not going to see this happen until WE do what God has told us to do! No wonder we are not seeing revival yet. Pride has us setting in our sanctified seats on Sundays and we think "I'm ok, you're ok, we are all ok?" Really? Who says we are?

These statistics will change, but at present, did you know Christian men between 18 and 20 years old are particularly striking? 77% look at pornography monthly. 36% view pornography on a daily basis. Over 40 million Americans are regular viewers to porn sites. [The research studies, primarily by the Barna Group. The "Missions Frontiers" website posted an article on this November-December 2020 issue Human Trafficking The Church Should Stop Supporting It!" Public Information]

We desperately need a revival. We need a move of God that will rock us all to the core. Our pious smug church masks are an abomination to God. He sees it all and He specifically says exam your HEART (your emotions, thoughts, and inner man), because your HEAD will tell you, you are ok! In other words, you will convince yourself that you are ok as the enemy of your soul whispers those lies into your thoughts.

No Church! We are NOT ok! When we have some church leaders in America who tell their married couples its ok to view pornography together in the privacy of your own bedroom, and use things that are appalling to God on the marriage bed, these leaders are dragging men and women to divorce courts and some to hell, why? Because many of them have become confused by their leaders, they have left the church and walked away from it all, and sad to say some of these "leaders' just do not care! God help us ALL!

There is SIN IN THE CAMP and it has to GO or our country will continue to sink deeper and deeper and deeper into despair. Why can't the church world see this? Why are they allowing themselves to be dragged like sheep to the slaughter swallowing everything hook, line, and sinker?

The deceiver is on the move and doing a pretty good job of convincing many that there is no heaven and there is no hell. So just live the way you want to. It is a LIE! LIES are EVERYWHERE and people are being deceived by these lies. WAKE UP CHURCH before it is TOO LATE! God's Word is clear and says, "...But the cowardly, unbelieving, abominable, murderers, sexually immoral, sorcerers, idolaters, and *ALL LIARS* shall have their part in the lake which burns with fire and brimstone, which is the second death." (Revelation 21:8 NKJV)

To repent means to apologize to God, ask Him for forgiveness for grieving Him with our sinful ways. We need to see Jesus in our minds eye and picture ourselves looking at Him in the face. Does He not say to seek Him? This is where we start.

1. We must truly repent and be broken before God for the sin we actively have been involved in
2. We must fall on our faces in humility before a Holy and Pure God!
3. Then we must turn from our sin and go the opposite direction from that sin. What we can't do on our own, the Holy Spirit will be there to help us.

"If we boast that we have no sin, we're only fooling ourselves and are strangers to the truth. But if we freely admit our sins when His light uncovers them, He will be faithful to forgive us every time. **God is just to forgive us our sins** because of Christ, and He will continue to cleanse us from all unrighteousness. If we claim that we're not guilty of sin when God uncovers it with His light, we make Him a liar and His Word is not in us." (I John 1:8-9 TPT)

Jesus is coming whether you want to believe it or not. If you do not believe it, He will come anyway. Your unbelief is not going to stop Him from coming! You have undoubtedly heard the phrase, "Get right, or Get left." The time for playing these church games are over. The world can see right through us, and many have turned away from 'the church.' They want to see people who talk it, walk it, and live it! Get your heart right with God before it is too late. Jesus IS coming again. He sees the sin people are hiding in their hearts. He is not playing the hide and seek game. He is saying, "Ready or not, I AM COMING!"

People who go to church, you have no idea what the person next to you is struggling with. You might be surprised. It might be an addiction. But Jesus came to break those chains off and bring true freedom to all who repent and turn from their habit. No matter whether that addiction is food, sexual addictions, porn addictions, cussing addiction, drugs and alcoholic addictions, marital affair addictions, and on and on and on. Get free! It is a horrible being caught in Satan's trap and devices, only God can break you free. Only God! Pray right now and get right with God. Turn away from that thing that grieves the heart of God.

There ARE some very good, God-fearing pastors, leaders, and churches still out there. Connect with them. Connect with people who will walk you through to your freedom, who will not condemn you, but will embrace you with the love of the Lord. "For ALL have sinned and fall short of the glory of God..." (Romans 3:23 NKJV) So you are not alone.

As you have read this book and found that soldiers are strong in the power of God's might. Understand that we are weakened by the state of sin. Know that it is a must to be right with God so that the power of God can flow through you, as you go out to win those who have fallen to the prey of the enemy of their soul.

As we send troops out who are right with God and close to His heart, who have pure motives, you can and WILL see a mighty move of God as you put into action God's Biblical Strategy for Revival in your city. There is power in multiplication. If you already evangelize or have outreach in your ministry, take it to the next level. Raise up an Army of the Lord! Fight the good fight! Win the lost and set captives free. As a soldier of the cross you have the proper equipment, you have now been trained, you can go out in the power and strength of the Lord and reach your community for Christ. As you keep being faithful you are equipped to Start a Revival in Your City! Multiply your efforts and raise up an ARMY OF THE LORD! Spread the word to other ministries you may know. Encourage them to raise up and Army of the Lord in their ministry too! Remember, there is no competition! We are all one working together to build the Kingdom of God!

A devouring fire cannot be contained. It will consume everything that stands in its path. The more it consumes the hotter the fire gets. This also is a powerful example of revival! "For our God is a consuming fire." (Hebrews 12:29 NKJV) A heaven sent, heaven directed, fire, from God Himself. He will fan the flames. As He does, church programs, methods, agendas, committees will burn under the flames of a true, authentic move of God, a powerful, real revival. Let God be God and watch as He will devour everything the fire is near. When this fire of God falls it will consume everything in its path just as it did in the story of Elijah as we read in (I Kings 18 NKJV). God will rush through your church, community, city, state and then go out into the nations. This revival is not just for a selected few, this NEW revival is for whosoever will. Your life will be devoured by God and your life will cease to be your own. The passion of God will consume you. You will find yourself completely consumed by God's presence and power. You will have a zeal for God's house and for lost souls and for more of God like never before. You will feel the Holy Spirit carry you as the winds begin to blow fresh upon the flames of revival. Your every thought will be consumed by God. A TRUE REVIVAL is intense!

As your troops go out under the fresh fire anointed by God's Spirit, it won't be long before your city is on fire for God. Bars will be vacant, streets will be silent from the vandals and murderers as God gets ahold of their hearts and changes them in the likeness of Jesus. As in the day of Elijah, let the fire on God's altar consume everything that is unpleasing and not of Him.

Soldiers, God has commanded us, His people, to cross the angry waters unafraid in these most perilous times. Put your feet in troubled waters and watch for a miracle. Life's experiences have flooded the banks of people's lives, and God is sending you forth as a mighty army! Ready for battle. The harvest and revival are on the very near horizon. As a soldier of the cross, be willing to go into the turbulent times, keep your eyes on Jesus and follow God's presence as you go. A mighty harvest awaits your arrival. A "God Invasion" will be released on your city by a mighty Army of the Lord. God will use them to release a mighty invasion of God's awesome presence and power on your city! Now go START A REVIVAL IN YOUR CITY!

"When you go out to fight your enemies and you face horses and chariots and an army greater than your own, do not be afraid. The Lord your God, who brought you out of the land of Egypt, is with you! When you prepare for battle the priest must come forward to speak to the troops. He will say to them, 'Listen to me, all you men of Israel! Do not be afraid as you go out to fight your enemies today! Do not lose heart or panic or tremble before them. For the Lord your God is going with you! He will fight for you against your enemies, and He will give you victory!" (Deuteronomy 20:1-4 NLT)

THE OATH OF COMMITMENT

"I, _____ have this day, voluntarily enlisted myself, as a soldier, in the Army of the Lord. I commit myself to giving full attention to the teaching and the training provided and will complete all classes and class assignments. I commit myself to God and my leaders to take this opportunity seriously. I understand the importance to be fully trained in this program, so that I can be spiritually equipped to be effective in this ministry as unto God. I commit to serve God and His Kingdom in following the guidance and direction of my spiritual leaders in the Army of the Lord. I will commit to living a lifestyle that is pleasing to the Lord, and volunteer my service to help this ministry in any way possible to help usher people into the Kingdom of God. I will support this ministry in every means possible to help further the gospel of the Lord Jesus Christ to see souls saved. I solemnly commit myself before God and this ministry, that I will serve well and faithfully the opportunities of which I am about to enter, so help me God."

Signature _____

Date _____

MORE ABOUT THE AUTHOR

In 2013 I believe God spoke a very clear word to my heart, "Karyl, I want you to start an intercession group of prayer for revival and call it "God Invasion". We put together a group for the purpose of seeing if others felt the same need and would join us. In September of 2013 in Gaffney, South Carolina we had our first gathering. We brought in a special speaker and were happy that we had 120 people attend, the same number of people as was in the Upper Room. In October 2013 we moved to another location in Spartanburg, South Carolina and again had 120 people come, and the Holy Spirit moved powerfully. The people asked if we could have another one the following month, so we went back to Gaffney, South Carolina and saw some continued growth.

Holidays were upon us, so we felt to stop until God led us in the next move. We waited on the Lord for one year, seeking Him for what His instructions and direction would be this new ministry. On September 11,2015 we ventured to meet at a place in Greenville, South Carolina where a pastor gave us his facility to use, free of charge. He only needed Sunday morning and Wednesday nights. We had 7 in attendance when we started, so we began to pray for God's direction for God Invasion in the coming New Year. October and November the group began to grow from 7 to 35 people, then the holiday's season again caused us to wait. Prayer is our number one focus, always!!!

Just days before Christmas I felt the Holy Spirit speak very clearly to my heart. He said, "I want you to bring in national speakers that I lead you to for the first weekend of every month for one year." I knew that it was God. In faith I immediately wrote emails to twenty well known revival speakers whose names I saw in a Christian Magazine, and by December 24, six had responded to my invitation and half of our new year was lined up with anointed men and women of God.

In January 2016 we began our new ministry with a 21 Day Fast. It was so effective we continue to do so to this day. We found it sets the tone for the whole year. In February we launched our Grand Opening. Our first speaker spoke on "Re-Digging the Wells of Revival." He spoke about revivals that had taken place in North and South Carolina. One of those places was Holmes Bible College where a revival had taken place on the top of Paris Mountain, S.C a 100 years ago. After the Saturday morning session, he asked for our core team of intercessors to join his team to go to the top of Paris Mountain to reclaim revival in South Carolina, North Carolina, and Georgia. For two and a half hours we prayed on that mountain and claimed revival to come as far as we could see. We asked God to open up revivals to all who were interceding, praying, and believing for an authentic move of God to come. At the conclusion we had communion and dedicated the mountain back to God. In March our guest speaker was known for having an anointing for "Breaking Strongholds off of families over regions, churches, ministries, and households." Following the weekend session, we felt to go back to Paris Mountain one more time. We asked the speaker who agreed to go with us, along with seven intercessors back up to Paris Mountain to break strongholds that were hovering over the entire region. When we reached the top of the mountain he said, "the scripture that comes to my mind is "Lift up your heads, O you gates! And be lifted up, you everlasting doors! And the King of glory shall come in. Who is this King of glory? The Lord strong and mighty, The Lord mighty in battle. Lift up your heads, O you gates! Lift up, you everlasting doors! And the King of glory shall come in. Who is this King of glory? The Lord of hosts, He is the King of glory." (Psalm 24:7-10 NKJV). He told us to shout three times, "Welcome, Welcome, Welcome to the King of Kings and Lord of Lords". When he blew his shofar we all felt, 'mission accomplished'. We felt that was the conclusion of our mandate for Paris Mountain. After we had gone up the last time in March 2016, a few of our people decided to go back up to the mountain on their own. They came back and reported to us, that the city officials had come and put a gate across the entrance of the road going up to the mountain. *No one* could any longer go up past that point. We felt that God sealed the work that He had done!

Throughout the whole year, it became apparent that every speaker God had lined up had been sent directly by Him. Every message had laid the foundation for this ministry in preparation for revival. At the conclusion of 2016, the foundation for God Invasion had been strategically laid.

All the messages over the year included "Re-Digging the Wells of Revival, Breaking Down Strongholds over the Region, Stirring the Waters of Revival, The Sovereignty of God and the Power of Prayer and Intercession. Elements of Revival to prepare hearts for the coming move of God. In July we had a City-Wide Outreach Event and the last night we had a move of God and young people literally got up from their seats and were running to the altar for salvation. The last three months messages on were about signs, wonders, and miracles, keep praying, and to be faithful in prayer and intercession that revival would come. At the close of the year our guest speaker was someone who had been mentored by the well-known revivalist and evangelist Steve Hill, from the Brownsville Revival in Pensacola, Florida.

As we concluded the year 2016, we could clearly see that God had strategically ordained every speaker He had sent to God Invasion. They all were directed and anointed by God, and the foundation was established.

Another amazing thing that happened was when we began, we had only $800.00 in our bank account. We took a huge step of faith when we invited these national speakers, we believed God would provide, because we knew God was leading us. Of course, this meant accommodations, flights, meals, offerings for the speakers, and we were a brand-new ministry! I can tell you; every month God met every need and never to this day have we ever been in lack, He has always provided.

I felt it very necessary to lay the foundation of our ministry to readers who have possibly never heard of us. PRAYER is our foundation and always will be. Our vision, purpose, and plan have been very clear and continues to be to this day.

God Invasion is a strategic part of birthing and releasing an authentic move of God resulting in a Great Awakening in many churches, cities, and nations.

We are a Revival Movement that exists to equip and empower a mighty new generation of leaders and people who will be catalysts for revival in their churches, parachurch ministries, schools, colleges, and the marketplace.

We have God Invasion Revival Hubs. These are identified and established by pastors under God Invasion, who feel a leading to establish a God Invasion and explosion of revival in their city. They contact God Invasion and the new revival prayer hubs plans are developed and implemented.

When we unite as one, an atmosphere is ignited and with prayer, anointed music, and the Word of God, people are ignited by the Spirit of God. When this happens, people become carriers of the fresh fire back to their cities, hubs, ministries.

When Covid-19 hit our nation in 2020, it immobilized many of us for a season, as it did many. During that time, we did two 21 Day Fasts. We sought God for the next move for this ministry. We kept feeling in our spirit to not go back to the old, that the foundation of this ministry had been laid. We also knew that God had said in His word, "Thus says the Lord, who makes a way in the sea And a path through the mighty waters, Who brings forth the chariot and horse, and THE ARMY and the POWER...Do not remember the former things, nor consider the things of old. Behold, I will do a new thing, now it shall spring forth; shall you not know it?" (Isaiah 43:16-17a-18a NKJV)

While seeking the Lord late one evening, I suddenly felt impressed to pray, "God, we do not know what the "New Thing" is. But I feel it is just that, "NEW", so what is my part in this "New Thing?" Thousands upon thousands are praying for revival all over the world. But, the truth is, none of us knows how to bring it. We are praying but not seeing the results that we are praying for. I need you to show me "how" if you want me to be a part of releasing a revival. What is this "NEW" and how do we obtain it?"

Immediately He began to pour what I consider to be divine direction into my spirit, and this book is a direct result of that prayer. I felt Him say, "Seek Me for My Biblical Strategy for Revival and I will give you the NEW THING! Ideas and thoughts started pouring into my mind. I got up and wrote as fast as I could and that is where this all began. He said, "raise up an ARMY of the Lord!" God literally led me to a group in a restaurant who already were operating in uniform and were called the Army of the Lord. Confirmation! I asked if they had a manual and they said, "no." That motivated me with what God had already spoke to my heart.

Many who know me have already jumped into this NEW THING, they have purchased their uniforms and have 'signed up' to be in the Army of the Lord. We have a church whose pastor in Honduras has already signed up 20 or his people. We are moving forward. As this book goes out, we are praying for a revival to start in YOUR city!

There is a great war being raged in our nation and in our world today. As you have read, I am a firm and strong believer in prayer.

I have led intercession groups for years, written books on the "Prayer Power", and "God Invasion-Releasing Revival." I know in centuries past revivals, prayer has been the key. I still believe that it is!!! It has to be! It is the heart of the Father. He said He is "doing a "NEW thing", NOW it will spring forth!" That is the reason for this book. God has given us our NEW assignment, and I believe this can and will transform cities. God will raise up people in YOUR church, ministry, para-church ministry, schools, colleges, and marketplaces to win YOUR CITY for our Lord Jesus Christ, and together we will set our world on fire with the greatest revival our world has ever seen.

Thank you for taking the time to read this book and practical manual. May your hearts be encouraged and inspired to take this book to your people and challenge them to get out of the seats to win the harvest that awaits you in your city. We are praying for fires of revival to be lit in cities all over the world!!

You hold in your hands a book that will guide you step by step, as you lead your people to "Start A Revival In Your City." You have sown much seed into the hearts of your people with incredible teaching and preaching. They are ready NOW to work!!! All they need is for you to raise up an Army of the Lord in your CITY and watch what God will do. You now have the Biblical Strategy to go

START A REVIVAL IN YOUR CITY!

WE WOULD LOVE TO HEAR FROM YOU

If you are raising up an army of the lord

Let us know

We want to connect with you

We would enjoy seeing a picture of your troop

TELL US ABOUT YOUR MINISTRY

Name, City, State, or Country

Let's Get Acquainted

Together We Can Make a Difference!

Let's WIN our World and Build God's Kingdom Together!

Thank you for joining us!

Email us at: godinvasion@usa.com

OTHER BOOKS AVAILABLE

By

KARYL GAEHRING

www.amazon.com

Prayer power

God Invasion – Releasing Revival

Help God! I'm a Pastor's Wife

*Is Heaven Real?

*Is God Real?

*An Evangelism Tool

---

i3D CLUB CURRICULUM

A One Year Faith Based Drug Prevention Program

ONLY SOLD IN THESE TWO PLACES

www.i3dclub.org

www.amazon.com

*Be sure to watch the 1 min. 30 sec. Video for more information

KARYL GAEHRING
IS AVAILABLE TO SPEAK

Churches

Revival Meetings

Conferences

Outreach Ministries

Para-Church Ministries

Retreats

Tent Revivals

For Bookings

karylgaehring@usa.com

References Available Upon Request

Made in the USA
Columbia, SC
04 July 2023